Get Going *with* Grammar

Games for practising grammar

Jennifer Meldrum
Barbara Reimer

Garnet
EDUCATION

Published by
Garnet Publishing Ltd.
8 Southern Court, South Street,
Reading RG1 4QS, UK

Copyright © 2004 Garnet Publishing Ltd.

This edition first published 2004
Reprinted 2013

The right of Jennifer Meldrum and Barbara Reimer
to be identified as the authors of this work has
been asserted by them in accordance with the
Copyright, Designs and Patents Act 1988.

British Library Cataloguing-in-Publication Data
A catalogue record for this book is available from
the British Library.

ISBN 978 1 85964 748 6

Production

Project manager:	Richard Peacock
Editorial team:	Francesca Pinagli,
	Lucy Thompson,
	Helen Blackwell
Art director:	David Rose
Design and typesetting:	Andrea Baker at
	IFA Design
Illustration:	Mark Tucker at
	IFA Design

Special thanks to Bob Reimer for unfailing
encouragement and technical advice.

Every effort has been made to trace the copyright
holders and we apologize in advance for any
unintentional omissions. We will be happy to insert
the appropriate acknowledgements in any
subsequent edition.

Printed and bound
in Lebanon by International Press:
interpress@int-press.com

Get Going with Grammar
Contents

Note from the Authors

We are excited about sharing these grammar games with you. Created specifically to encourage students to practise discrete grammar points, these games keep students focused on English language production. In teaching monolingual EFL classes, we have found that students tend to revert to their native language if the task is not specific enough. For this reason, our grammar games require students to use specific language skills. These games are valuable in a hetero-linguistic ESL environment as well, because the common language is still English.

In addition, there is a built-in adaptability component to these games. In our teaching experience, we have often searched through game books for an activity to review grammar elements, only to find that the prepared game doesn't emphasize exactly what we have taught. With our book, you can use the game provided or play one of the suggested variations. Also, for many of our games we have provided templates, which allow you to make your own versions.

We hope that these games will assist you in the classroom, and provide many hours of enjoyable learning for your students. We would love to hear about your experiences using them.

Notes on Preparation

Many games can be made "permanent" by laminating the boards and cards or mounting them on cardboard. For **place markers**, you can use coins, bottle caps, buttons, coloured plastic pieces or coloured paper clips.

If you do not have **dice**, you can use number boards instead. When it is a student's turn to roll the die, the student closes his eyes and points his finger (or a pencil) on the board. The number he is touching is the number of spaces he moves. The other students in the group watch to ensure the student is not "choosing" the number he wants. When a student lands between numbers, the other students in the group judge which number is closest. Give one board to each group instead of a die. Change the boards from time to time. We have included a sheet of number boards for photocopying.

Number Boards

Board 1

```
6 3 2 1 4 5 3 2 6 1
1 4 5 4 3 6 1 4 2 3
2 5 6 3 1 4 2 6 5 6
5 1 3 2 4 6 5 3 2 4
4 6 1 5 3 2 4 5 6 1
3 2 5 1 4 3 6 1 4 5
2 5 3 6 1 4 5 3 2 1
1 4 2 3 5 6 3 1 6 4
6 3 5 4 1 2 4 3 5 2
3 6 4 1 2 5 6 2 1 3
```

Board 2

```
2 1 6 5 3 4 2 6 1 5
1 3 5 4 1 2 6 5 2 3
6 4 2 1 6 3 5 2 6 4
3 5 1 3 2 6 4 1 5 2
5 2 6 4 5 1 3 6 4 5
2 1 4 3 1 5 6 4 1 3
4 6 3 2 5 1 4 5 6 2
2 3 1 5 6 4 2 3 4 5
1 4 2 6 3 5 1 6 2 3
6 5 4 3 2 1 3 2 4 6
```

Board 3

```
3 2 5 6 1 4 3 1 6 5
5 6 4 1 3 6 5 2 4 1
1 3 5 2 4 1 6 1 3 5
4 1 6 3 5 1 2 6 5 4
2 4 1 4 2 3 1 3 1 2
6 5 2 5 6 2 4 5 2 3
5 1 3 4 1 5 3 4 1 6
2 3 6 2 6 3 2 6 2 3
1 4 5 3 4 5 1 5 4 1
5 6 3 4 2 1 6 3 6 2
```

Board 4

```
3 6 5 1 4 2 6 5 3 1
1 4 2 4 6 3 1 4 5 6
5 2 3 6 1 4 5 3 2 3
2 1 6 5 4 3 2 6 5 4
4 3 1 2 6 5 4 2 3 1
6 5 2 1 4 6 3 1 4 2
5 2 6 3 1 4 2 6 5 1
1 4 5 6 2 3 6 1 3 4
3 6 2 4 1 5 4 6 2 5
6 3 4 1 5 2 3 5 1 6
```

Board 5

```
2 6 1 4 3 5 2 1 6 4
6 3 4 5 6 2 1 4 2 3
1 5 2 6 1 3 4 2 1 5
3 4 6 3 2 1 5 6 4 2
4 2 1 5 4 6 3 1 5 4
2 6 5 3 6 4 1 5 6 3
5 1 3 2 4 6 5 4 1 2
2 3 6 4 1 5 2 3 5 4
6 5 2 1 3 4 6 1 2 3
1 4 5 3 2 6 3 2 5 1
```

Board 6

```
1 2 4 6 3 5 1 3 6 4
4 6 5 3 1 6 4 2 5 3
3 1 4 2 5 3 6 3 1 4
5 3 6 1 4 3 2 6 4 5
2 5 3 5 2 1 3 1 3 2
6 4 2 4 6 2 5 4 2 1
4 3 1 5 3 4 1 5 3 6
2 1 6 2 6 1 2 6 2 1
3 5 4 1 5 4 3 4 5 3
4 6 1 5 2 3 6 1 6 2
```

Board 7

```
2 3 6 5 4 1 3 6 2 5
5 4 1 4 3 2 5 4 6 3
6 1 2 3 5 4 6 2 1 2
1 5 3 6 4 2 1 3 6 4
4 2 5 1 3 6 4 1 2 5
3 6 1 5 4 3 2 5 4 1
6 1 3 2 5 4 1 3 6 5
5 4 6 3 1 2 3 5 2 4
2 3 1 4 5 6 4 3 1 6
3 2 4 5 6 1 2 6 5 3
```

Board 8

```
3 1 5 6 2 4 3 5 1 6
1 2 6 4 1 3 5 6 3 2
5 4 3 1 5 2 6 3 5 4
2 6 1 2 3 5 4 1 6 3
6 3 5 4 6 1 2 5 4 6
3 1 4 2 1 6 5 4 1 2
4 5 2 3 6 1 4 6 5 3
3 2 1 6 5 4 3 2 4 6
1 4 3 5 2 6 1 5 3 2
5 6 4 2 3 1 2 3 4 5
```

Board 9

```
4 2 1 6 5 3 4 5 6 1
1 6 3 5 4 6 1 2 3 5
5 4 1 2 3 5 6 5 4 1
3 5 6 4 1 5 2 6 1 3
2 3 5 3 2 4 5 4 5 2
6 1 2 1 6 2 3 1 2 4
1 5 4 3 5 1 4 3 5 6
2 4 6 2 6 4 2 6 2 4
5 3 1 4 3 1 5 1 3 5
1 6 4 3 2 5 6 4 6 2
```

Quantifier Quest

Learning objective: To display knowledge of quantifiers by selecting the appropriate quantifier for the sentence on the game board.

Game objective: To be the first player to use all his/her cards or to arrive back at the Start square after going once around the board.

Organization: Played in small groups.

Preparation:
1. Copy one deck of cards and one game board for each group.
2. Provide a die for each group and a place marker for each student.

Description of the game: The deck of cards is shuffled, and each player receives six cards. In turn, each student throws a die and moves the corresponding number of spaces. He/She then tries to complete the sentence on the game board using one of the quantifier cards he/she has in his/her hand. If the sentence is correct, the student takes a new card from the deck, and play passes to the next student. If the sentence is incorrect, or a logical sentence cannot be made, the student takes two cards from the deck as a penalty. Play continues until all the cards have been played, or until no further correct sentences can be made.

Rules:
1. Deal six cards to each player.
2. The first student to play rolls a die, moves the corresponding number of spaces and tries to make a sentence using one of his/her quantifier cards.
3. If you make a correct sentence, take a new card from the deck and let the next student play.
4. If the match is incorrect, take two new cards from the deck as a penalty, and let the next student play.
5. You can challenge a sentence made by another student. If the sentence is incorrect, the student returns to the original square and takes the two cards as a penalty.
6. Play continues until all the cards are played, no correct sentences can be made, or a player arrives back at the <u>Start</u> square <u>after going once around the board</u>.

Note: Blank boards have been provided on pages 10 and 11 for you or groups of students to create new *Quantifier Quest* boards.

Quantifier Quest

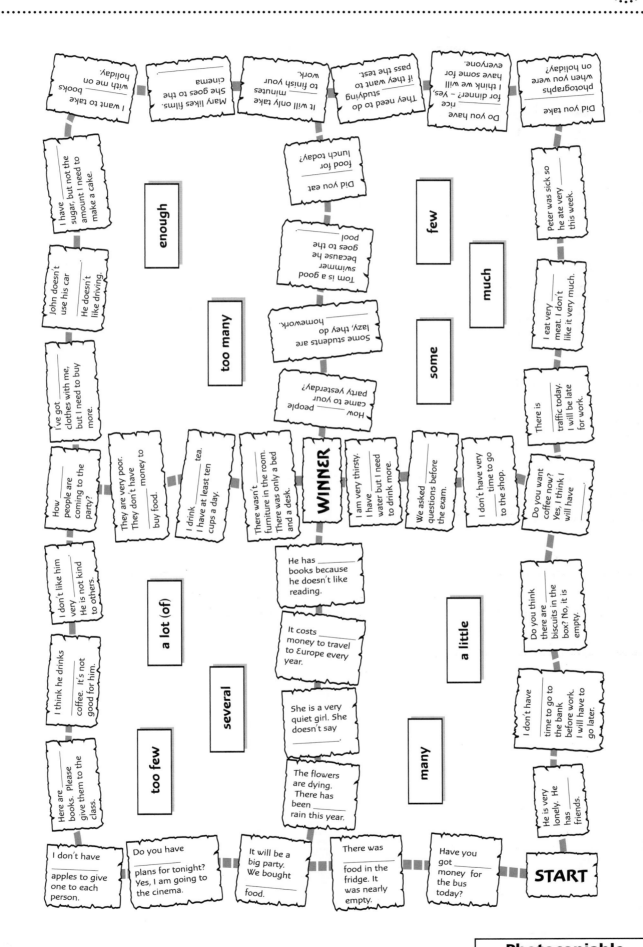

I want to take ____ books with me on holiday.

Mary likes films. She goes to the cinema ____.

It will only take ____ minutes to finish your work.

They need to do ____ studying if they want to pass the test.

Do you have ____ rice for dinner? – Yes, I think we will have some for everyone.

Did you take ____ photographs when you were on holiday?

I have ____ sugar, but not the ____ amount I need to make a cake.

enough

Did you eat ____ food for lunch today?

Tom is a good swimmer because he goes to the pool ____.

few

Peter was sick so he ate very ____ this week.

John doesn't use his car ____. He doesn't like driving.

too many

Some students are lazy, they do ____ homework.

some

much

I eat very ____ meat. I don't like it very much.

I've got ____ clothes with me, but I need to buy more.

How ____ people came to your party yesterday?

There is ____ traffic today. I will be late for work.

How ____ people are coming to the party?

They are very poor. They don't have ____ money to buy food.

I drink ____ tea. I have at least ten cups a day.

There wasn't ____ furniture in the room. There was only a bed and a desk.

WINNER

I am very thirsty. I have ____ water but I need to drink more.

We asked ____ questions before the exam.

I don't have very ____ time to go to the shop.

Do you want coffee now? Yes, I think I will have ____.

I don't like him very ____. He is not kind to others.

He has ____ books because he doesn't like reading.

Do you think there are ____ biscuits in the box? No, it is empty.

a lot (of)

It costs ____ money to travel to Europe every year.

a little

I think he drinks ____ coffee. It's not good for him.

She is a very quiet girl. She doesn't say ____.

I don't have ____ time to go to the bank before work. I will have to go later.

several

Here are ____ books. Please give them to the class.

The flowers are dying. There has been ____ rain this year.

many

He is very lonely. He has ____ friends.

too few

I don't have ____ apples to give one to each person.

Do you have ____ plans for tonight? Yes, I am going to the cinema.

It will be a big party. We bought ____ food.

There was ____ food in the fridge. It was nearly empty.

Have you got ____ money for the bus today?

START

Quantifier Quest – Cards

some	some	many	much	few
some	any	many	much	few
some	any	many	much	too few
some	any	many	much	a few
some	any	many	much	a few

Quantifier Quest – Cards

enough	a lot of	too many	too much	little
enough	a lot of	too many	too much	little
enough	a lot of	too many	too much	too little
enough	a lot of	too many	too much	a little
enough	a lot of	too many	too much	a little

Quantifier Quest – Template

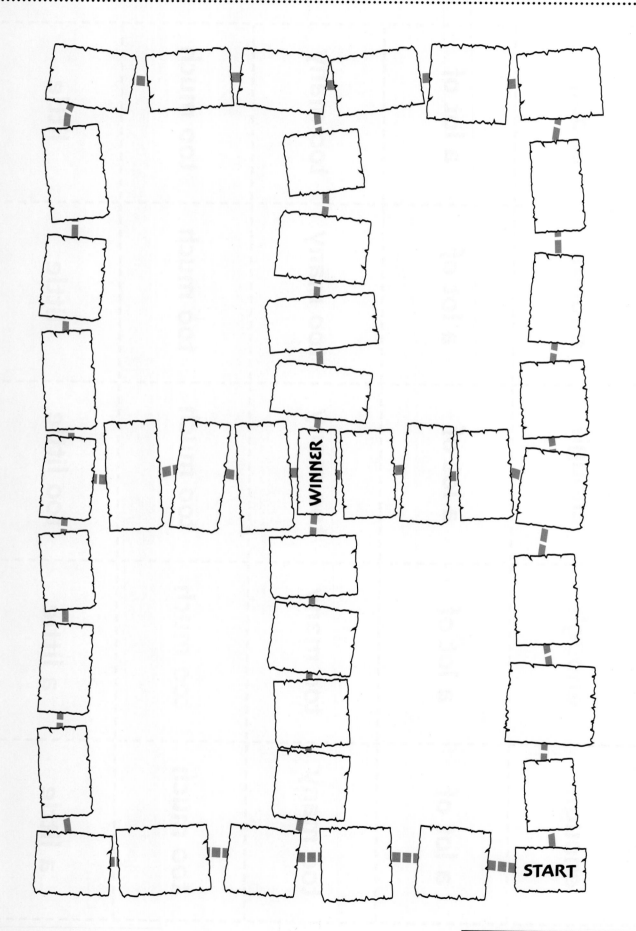

WINNER

START

Photocopiable

How Often Do You Think About Me?

Learning objective: To make sentences with adverbs of frequency.

Game objective: To try to guess correctly how often other students in the class do things. The student with the most matches wins.

Organization: Played in small groups of 3–4 students.

Preparation: Copy one survey sheet for each student.

Description of the game: Students fill in the chart labelled <u>Self</u> by ticking the box under the appropriate adverb of frequency. Each student should keep his/her answers a secret by folding the top of the paper over so no one can see what he/she has answered. Then the students fill in a similar chart for each member of the group by <u>guessing</u>. They do not ask the other students at this time.

After the students have filled in the charts for all members of the group, they take turns telling the others how they answered for the other members of the group. For example, everyone explains how they answered for Chris by saying, *I think Chris always takes a shower because he is always clean*, etc. After the students in the group have explained how they answered for Chris (using a sentence with an adverb of frequency), Chris tells the group how he answered for himself (again using a sentence with an adverb of frequency). When a student guesses correctly for another member of the group, he/she wins a point for each sentence he/she guessed correctly.

Rules:
1. Fold the top of the paper on the fold line so no one can see your answers for the <u>Self</u> box .
2. Put an X in the box under the adverb that is true for you.
3. Guess about the other members of your group. Do not ask them! Place your answers in the other charts.
4. When everyone has filled in all the charts, share your answers.
5. Choose one student. Everyone in the group tells the other students what answer they gave for one student. For example, tell Chris, *I think Chris always takes a shower because he is always clean. And Chris never eats chocolate because he is so thin.*
6. After all the students tell what answers they gave for "Chris", Chris tells the group what answer he really has. If you guessed correctly, you win a point.
7. Do the same for all students in the group.
8. The student with the most correct guesses wins!

Variation:
- There are blank boards on pages 14 and 15 to write in different verb phrases or different adverbs of frequency.

WARNING: What makes this game fun is the potential teasing students can do with each other. The more controversial the questions, the more fun students have. However, it also has potential to hurt sensitive students' feelings. Therefore, this game can only be played in a supportive classroom environment, and it is better if students can make their own groups rather than assigning them, even if it means more groups of smaller numbers.

How Often Do You Think About Me?

- (fold line) -

Self:

	always	usually	sometimes	rarely	never
have a shower					
eat chocolate					
call my mother					
spend money					
make mistakes					
study English					

Student 2:

	always	usually	sometimes	rarely	never
has a shower					
eats chocolate					
calls his/her mother					
spends money					
makes mistakes					
studies English					

Number correct: _____

Student 3:

	always	usually	sometimes	rarely	never
has a shower					
eats chocolate					
calls his/her mother					
spends money					
makes mistakes					
studies English					

Number correct: _____

Student 4:

	always	usually	sometimes	rarely	never
has a shower					
eats chocolate					
calls his/her mother					
spends money					
makes mistakes					
studies English					

Number correct: _____

How Often Do You Think About Me? – Template

- (fold line) -

Self:

Student 2:

Number correct: _____

Student 3:

Number correct: _____

Student 4:

Number correct: _____

How Often Do You Think About Me?

You're It, Aren't You?

Learning objective: To practise adding the correct tag question to a statement.

Game objective: To play all of the cards in a student's hand before other students play their cards.

Organization: Played in small groups of 3–5 students.

Preparation:
1. Copy a board and a set of tag ending cards for each group.
2. Provide a die for each group and a place marker for each student.

Optional: Copy the rules sheet for each group or put the rules on the board.

Description of the game: Each small group of students mixes the tag ending cards and distributes them equally to each student in the group. Extra cards are set aside. Each student places his/her place marker in any shaded corner space. In turn, each student rolls a single die and moves in any direction, looking for a square that will allow him/her to play a tag ending card from his/her hand. The first part of the question is in the squares on the board. The second part is on each card. The sentence must be correct grammatically. For example, to play a card that reads *aren't they?*, the student may land on the space marked *The children are cute* or *They are hungry*. If a student lands on a space where he/she is unable to play a card, he/she forfeits his/her turn. The first student to play all of his/her cards wins.

Rules:
1. Begin by placing your marker on any one of the four shaded corner spaces.
2. Roll the die and move in any direction. The space must touch horizontally or vertically – <u>not diagonally</u>.
3. You <u>must</u> land on the space in an exact die roll. If you roll '3', you must move <u>three</u> spaces, not two or one.
4. If you do not have a card to finish the sentence begun in the space, you must wait for your next turn to play again.
5. If you have a card to finish the sentence begun in the space, read the complete tag question and place your card face down on the table.
6. If you make an incorrect tag question and the other students tell you, you may not put your card down and you lose your next turn.

Variation:
• There are three different boards with matching tag ending cards.

You're It, Aren't You?

Rules:
1. Begin by placing your marker on any one of the four shaded corner spaces.
2. Roll the die and move in any direction. The space must touch horizontally or vertically – not diagonally.
3. You must land on the space in an exact die roll. If you roll '3', you must move three spaces, not two or one.
4. If you do not have a card to finish the sentence begun in the space, you must wait for your next turn to play again.
5. If you have a card to finish the sentence begun in the space, read the complete tag question and place your card face down on the table.
6. If you make an incorrect tag question and the other students tell you, you may not put your card down and you lose your next turn.

Rules:
1. Begin by placing your marker on any one of the four shaded corner spaces.
2. Roll the die and move in any direction. The space must touch horizontally or vertically – not diagonally.
3. You must land on the space in an exact die roll. If you roll '3', you must move three spaces, not two or one.
4. If you do not have a card to finish the sentence begun in the space, you must wait for your next turn to play again.
5. If you have a card to finish the sentence begun in the space, read the complete tag question and place your card face down on the table.
6. If you make an incorrect tag question and the other students tell you, you may not put your card down and you lose your next turn.

Rules:
1. Begin by placing your marker on any one of the four shaded corner spaces.
2. Roll the die and move in any direction. The space must touch horizontally or vertically – not diagonally.
3. You must land on the space in an exact die roll. If you roll '3', you must move three spaces, not two or one.
4. If you do not have a card to finish the sentence begun in the space, you must wait for your next turn to play again.
5. If you have a card to finish the sentence begun in the space, read the complete tag question and place your card face down on the table.
6. If you make an incorrect tag question and the other students tell you, you may not put your card down and you lose your next turn.

Rules:
1. Begin by placing your marker on any one of the four shaded corner spaces.
2. Roll the die and move in any direction. The space must touch horizontally or vertically – not diagonally.
3. You must land on the space in an exact die roll. If you roll '3', you must move three spaces, not two or one.
4. If you do not have a card to finish the sentence begun in the space, you must wait for your next turn to play again.
5. If you have a card to finish the sentence begun in the space, read the complete tag question and place your card face down on the table.
6. If you make an incorrect tag question and the other students tell you, you may not put your card down and you lose your next turn.

You're It, Aren't You? – Cards

Present Tense

doesn't she?	doesn't she?	doesn't he?	doesn't he?	is it?	aren't they?	don't we?	are we?	isn't it?
does he?	aren't they?	does she?	isn't it?	isn't it?	aren't we?	isn't he?	isn't he?	doesn't she?
isn't he?	does she?	is it?	haven't you?	is he?	is it?	isn't it?	isn't it?	isn't he?
aren't they?	is it?	isn't he?	isn't she?	doesn't he?	are we?	don't you?	hasn't she?	isn't it?
don't you?	are we?	aren't we?	isn't it?	isn't she?	doesn't he?	aren't we?	isn't he?	doesn't she?
isn't she?	isn't it?	doesn't she?	doesn't he?	aren't they?	isn't it?	isn't he?	don't you?	doesn't she?
isn't it?	doesn't she?	isn't it?	aren't you?	does she?	isn't it?	don't you?	don't you?	isn't he?

You're It, Aren't You?

Present Tense

- The car is red,
- Ed needs a wife,
- Jill has three children,
- Judy is pregnant,
- The smoke is thick in here,
- Janey has a pet dog,
- Tim is a civil engineer,
- His wife cooks well,
- Peter isn't very tall,
- We are bringing games,
- Mary has a cat,
- The train isn't on time,
- The dogs are loud,
- You help me a lot,
- The children are cute,
- This computer isn't fast,
- English is easy to learn,
- Tom is absent today,
- Bill is lost in the school,
- Fred swims in a team,
- That actress is beautiful,
- May goes to every party,
- John is here today,
- Jennifer doesn't smoke,
- Joe is home tonight,
- Maria lives in Syria,
- Robert doesn't shave,
- Your watch is slow,
- The news isn't good,
- Chris doesn't drive,
- You paint very well,
- We aren't there yet,
- That teacher is good,
- We aren't going now,
- You have a good dentist,
- You are bringing the lemonade,
- We call him every night,
- The manager is nice,
- David comes late every day,
- The people are busy,
- We are going to the party,
- Barbara drives a car,
- The doctor is very attractive,
- The blackboard is clean,
- You have many classes,
- You play soccer,
- This game is easy,
- Sandy doesn't like me,
- The concert is excellent,
- John isn't very happy,
- Frank is a good student,
- You are a fast typist,
- We aren't eating there,
- That woman is pretty,
- The bus is later than usual,
- They are angry,
- Rick takes the bus to work,
- You play basketball,
- The weather is nice today,
- This class is interesting,
- Your aunt dances well,
- Nancy loves to read,
- You have this book,
- She reads in English,
- Laura has a job,
- We aren't going to the gym,
- They are hungry,

Present and Past Tense

isn't she?	did he?	wasn't he?	weren't they?	didn't you?	isn't she?	isn't it?
isn't she?	don't you?	is she?	is it?	are we?	wasn't it?	does she?
wasn't he?	does she?	is it?	wasn't he?	aren't we?	does she?	isn't it?
didn't he?	are we?	haven't you?	doesn't she?	is he?	didn't he?	wasn't it?
is it?	isn't it?	is he?	did he?	isn't it?	aren't they?	has she?
doesn't she?	weren't they?	does she?	aren't we?	didn't he?	aren't we?	isn't it?
isn't he?	wasn't he?	wasn't it?	wasn't he?	aren't we?	isn't he?	didn't you?
are we?	wasn't he?	wasn't he?	hasn't she?	hasn't she?	wasn't he?	aren't you?
aren't they?	hasn't she?	didn't he?	wasn't it?	wasn't it?	don't you?	doesn't she?

You're It, Aren't You?

Present and Past Tense

- The car was red,
- Ed got married last year,
- Jill has been to Mexico,
- Judy is pregnant,
- The smoke was thick there,
- Janey has seen this before,
- Tim was a civil engineer,
- His wife doesn't cook well,
- Peter isn't very tall,
- We are going to bring cups,
- Mike had an accident,
- The train isn't on time,
- The dogs were loud,
- You help me a lot,
- The children are cute,
- This computer isn't fast,
- English is easy to learn,
- Tom was absent yesterday,
- Bill was lost there,
- Fred used to swim in a team,
- That actress is beautiful,
- May isn't coming to my party,
- John was here yesterday,
- Barbara doesn't smoke,
- Joe was home last night,
- Maria lives in Syria,
- Robert didn't call,
- Your watch is slow,
- The news isn't good,
- Chris didn't play,
- You paint well,
- We aren't going to be late,
- That teacher was good,
- We are going now,
- You have been here before,
- You are bringing the lemonade,
- We are going to call him,
- The manager was nice,
- David came late,
- The people were busy,
- We aren't going to tell him,
- Jennifer drives a car,
- The doctor is very attractive,
- The blackboard was clean,
- You have tried this before,
- You used to play football,
- This game is easy,
- Sandy doesn't like me,
- The concert was good,
- John isn't very happy,
- Frank is a good student,
- You type fast,
- We are eating there,
- That woman is pretty,
- The bus is later than usual,
- They are angry,
- Rick drove to work,
- You used to play basketball,
- The weather is nice today,
- This class is interesting,
- Your aunt doesn't dance well,
- Nancy loves to read,
- You have been to France,
- She reads English,
- Laura has been to China,
- We aren't going yet,
- They are hungry,

Present Tense, Past Tense and Modals

isn't it?	isn't she?	didn't you?	weren't they?	wasn't he?	did he?	can't she?
can't you?	isn't it?	should we?	is it?	can she?	aren't they?	hasn't she?
isn't it?	does she?	shouldn't we?	does she?	is it?	doesn't she?	didn't he?
wasn't it?	didn't he?	is he?	can't she?	doesn't she?	weren't they?	didn't he?
can she?	aren't they?	isn't she?	did he?	wasn't he?	isn't it?	is it?
isn't it?	shouldn't we?	didn't he?	weren't they?	can she?	shouldn't we?	isn't she?
didn't you?	isn't he?	shouldn't we?	can't you?	wasn't it?	wasn't he?	should we?
can't you?	haven't you?	wasn't he?	hasn't she?	wasn't he?	wasn't he?	should we?
can't you?	didn't he?	haven't you?	wasn't it?	didn't he?	hasn't she?	aren't they?

You're It, Aren't You?

3.7

Present Tense, Past Tense and Modals

- The car was red,
- Ed got married last year,
- Jill has been to Mexico,
- Judy is pregnant,
- The smoke was thick there,
- Janey has seen this before,
- Tim was a civil engineer,
- His wife can't cook well,
- Peter isn't very tall,
- We should bring cups,
- Mike had an accident,
- The train isn't on time,
- The dogs were loud,
- You can help me,
- The children are cute,
- This computer isn't fast,
- English is easy to learn,
- Tom was absent yesterday,
- Bill was lost there,
- Fred used to swim in a team,
- That actress can sing,
- May can't come to my party,
- John was here yesterday,
- Barbara doesn't smoke,
- Joe was home last night,
- Maria lives in Syria,
- Robert didn't call,
- Your watch is slow,
- The news isn't good,
- Chris didn't play,
- You can paint,
- We shouldn't be late,
- That teacher was good,
- We should go now,
- You have been here before,
- You can bring the lemonade,
- We should call him,
- The manager was nice,
- David came late,
- The people were crowded,
- We shouldn't tell him,
- Jennifer can drive a car,
- The doctor is very attractive,
- The blackboard was clean,
- You have tried this before,
- You used to play football,
- This game is easy,
- Sandy doesn't like me,
- The concert was good,
- John isn't very happy,
- Frank is a good student,
- You can type fast,
- We should eat more fruit,
- That woman is pretty,
- The bus is later than usual,
- They are angry,
- Rick drove to work,
- You used to play basketball,
- The weather is nice today,
- This class is interesting,
- Your aunt can't dance,
- Nancy loves to read,
- You have been to France,
- She can't read English,
- Laura has been to China,
- We shouldn't go,
- They are hungry,

Photocopiable 23

Checkerboard Chatter

Learning objective: To practise forming the comparative and superlative forms of adjectives.

Game objective: To move the students' playing pieces to the opposite side of the board, retaining as many playing pieces as possible (as in standard checkers).

Organization: Played in pairs, or teams of two players.

Preparation:
1. Copy one board for each pair or group of students.
2. Provide 12 playing circles and a coin for each side. (Playing pieces are all the same colour for one side, and the two sides have different colours.)

Description of the game: In turn, each side moves a playing piece diagonally. After selecting the square, the player tosses the coin. If the coin lands on "heads", the student must form the comparative form of the adjective on which he/she has landed. If the coin lands on "tails", the student must form the superlative form of the adjective. If the form is correct, the player takes another turn. (The maximum number of consecutive turns is two.) If the form is incorrect, the player returns to the square from which he/she moved, and play passes to the other side. A player can jump a playing piece of the opponent by jumping and then making the applicable form of both the jumped square and the landing one, based on the coin toss. (Both forms must be correct in order to claim the square and remove the opponent's playing piece.) Play continues in turn, until all the pieces for one side have reached the other end of the board. The side with the most playing pieces remaining is the winner.

Rules:
1. Only one side plays at a time.
2. In turn, move a playing piece diagonally. After selecting the square, toss the coin.
3. If the coin lands on "heads", form the comparative form of the adjective on which you have landed. If the coin lands on "tails", form the superlative form of the adjective.
4. If the form is correct, have another turn. (The maximum number of consecutive turns is two.)
5. If the form is incorrect, return to the square from which you moved – play passes to the other side.
6. You can jump a playing piece of the opponent by jumping and then making the applicable form of both the jumped square and the landing one after the coin toss. (Both forms must be correct in order to claim the square and remove the opponent's playing piece.)
7. The other players judge the correctness of the form. (The teacher can judge, if necessary.)
8. After a maximum of two turns, play passes to the other side.
9. Play continues in turn, until all the pieces for one side have reached the other end of the board. The side with the most playing pieces remaining is the winner.

Variations:
- Have students make sentences with the word forms.
- Use the blank checkerboard template to practise any formation you choose.

Checkerboard Chatter

different	sad	pretty	new	difficult	comfortable	hot	hard
old	noisy	possible	warm	positive	high	near	logical
thin	expensive	white	easy	careful	fine	clear	dangerous
creative	sweet	careful	good	sleepy	obvious	common	small
ugly	slow	beautiful	full	important	poor	strong	attractive
interesting	clear	hungry	wonderful	young	blue	prominent	general
empty	special	soft	bad	slow	few	independent	short
capable	new	quick	friendly	afraid	narrow	long	simple

Checkerboard Chatter

Comparing Cards

Learning objective: To practise making comparative sentences.

Game objective: To play all of the cards in a student's hand.

Organization: Played in small groups of 3–5 students.

Preparation: Copy and cut a set of cards for each group.

Description of the game: Each small group of students mixes the cards together and distributes them equally to each student in the group. In turn, each student places a card from his/her hand and says a sentence comparing his/her card with the previous card. For example, if one player places *elephant*, another student can place *car* and say *A car is faster than an elephant.* Each adjective can only be used once within a group. So, once *faster* is used, it cannot be used again by anyone in the group. Play continues until there are no more cards left to play.

Rules:
1. Use the cards in your hand to make a comparative sentence. Compare your card with the card the student before you played.
2. One person in the group should write down the adjectives each player uses.
3. Each adjective can only be used once in a group. If someone else says *faster than*, then nobody else in the group may use *faster*.
4. If you cannot think of a sentence, you must pass your turn and not place a card.

Variations:
- Add a racing element by telling students they have five seconds to place their card and make a sentence. The other students time each other or have a timer. If a student cannot make a sentence in five seconds or repeats an adjective, he/she cannot play a card. The first person to play all of his/her cards wins.
- Give each small group the cards and have them make three-sentence sets with an adjective, comparative and superlative. For example: *A lion is big. A giraffe is bigger. An elephant is the biggest.* The team with the most correct three-sentence sets wins.

Comparing Cards

lion	giraffe	elephant	dog
cat	horse	fly	bird
chicken	fish	ice-cream	pizza
banana	apple	hamburger	cake
car	bicycle	yacht	motorcycle

Comparing Cards

aeroplane	train	house	tent
flower	sun	tree	mountain
television	stereo	computer	mobile phone
baby	grandmother	teacher	doctor
diamond ring	hammer	book	doll

Model Modals

Learning objective: To practise asking and answering questions with modals.

Game objective: To be the first to reach the end of the trail while asking and answering questions along the way.

Organization: Played in small groups of 3–5 students.

Preparation:
1. Copy one board for each group.
2. Provide a die for each group and a place marker for each student.

Description of the game: Students place their markers on the Start arrow. In turn, each student rolls the die and moves along the board. Students read the questions they land on. They must either ask a question, answer a question or ask another student to do something *Could you do me a favour?*. Students must use modals in their questions and answers.

Rules:
1. If you land on a question, you must answer the question using a modal.
2. If you land on a *May I ask you a question?* space, ask any student a question using a modal.
3. If you land on a *Could you do me a favour?* space, ask any student to do something for you (staying within the classroom), using a modal. Be polite!

Variation:
• Photocopy the board into an extra-large size or use an OHP to play the game in a small class.

Model Modals

START

What will you do this weekend?

What must you do to pass this class?

What can you do to help your family?

What would you do with a horse?

How should you treat a lady?

May I ask you a question?

What might you do next year?

What should you eat more?

Roll the die and move your marker. When you land on a space, read the question aloud and answer it honestly.

* When you land on *May I ask you a question?*, you may ask anyone else a question.
* When you land on *Could you do me a favour?*, you may ask anyone to do something for you.

What can a person see in your hometown?

When will you stop studying English?

How should you punish a child?

May I ask you a question?

How could a person learn faster?

What can you do really well?

How must you act at work?

How could you help your country?

What could you do to have more money?

What could you do tonight?

FINISH

Why should you take this game seriously?

How could a person stay happy?

How might you improve yourself?

Where will you eat dinner tomorrow?

What would you do with a new car?

What must a man do in a family?

Could you do me a favour?

Could you do me a favour?

What must you do in your job?

Could you do me a favour?

What must a woman do in a family?

Where might you go after class?

How could you be a better person?

How must a teacher act?

What will you do next week?

What can you do that is funny?

What should a son do for his father?

What do you wish you could do?

What might happen in the next class?

To whomf could you be nicer?

Who may be your friend after this class?

Use a modal in your answers and questions!
*You should be nice … you never can guess where your classmate will land next!

Where would you live if you were rich?

How could you be a better student?

Where might you live in 10 years' time?

What will you do if you pass this class?

May I ask you a question?

What might help you reach your goals?

What might stop you from achieving your goals?

Who may get the best grade in this class?

Talking Tenses

Learning objective: To practise a variety of verb tenses.

Game objective: To be the first person to play all of his/her cards correctly.

Organization: A group of 4–5 students is best, to maximize the number of turns and allow for adjudication of student answers, but you can work with a smaller or larger group, if desired.

Preparation: Copy the card sheets provided, giving one complete deck of cards to each group. (The deck consists of cards displaying various verb tenses.) There are also *Change Verb Tense* cards in the deck that allow the student to change from the current verb tense to another, if desired.

Description of the game: Each student is dealt five cards, face down. The remaining cards are placed face down in the middle of the circle, and the top card is turned over. This becomes the first verb tense to be played. If a *Change Verb Tense* card is turned over, the dealer can determine the first verb tense to be played. The student to the right of the dealer plays first. If the student has a verb tense card that corresponds to the verb tense in play, the student puts the card on top of the played cards, and makes a sentence using the verb on the card. The subject can be chosen by the player, provided it fits the verb form on the card (e.g., correct 3rd-person singular for the present tense). If the verb tense is correct, the subject matches the form, and the sentence is correct, the student draws another card and plays again. When the student has no more cards for that verb tense, no *Change Verb Tense* card, or makes an error, play passes to the next student.

Rules:
1. Deal five cards to each player, face down.
2. Place the remaining cards in the middle of the circle.
3. Turn over the top card on the deck to determine the first verb tense and put it beside the deck.
4. The student to the right of the dealer plays first. Only one student plays at a time.
5. If you have a verb tense card in your hand that corresponds to the verb tense in play, put the card on top of the play card beside the deck, and make a sentence using the verb on the card. You can choose a subject to fit the verb form.
6. The other players judge the correctness of the sentence. (The teacher can judge, if necessary.)
7. If the verb tense is correct, the subject matches the form, and the sentence is correct, draw another card and play again. If the sentence is incorrect, withdraw the played card and take a penalty card from the deck.
8. You can use a *Change Verb Tense* card at any time to change the verb tense that is in play.
9. When you have no more cards for that verb tense, no *Change Verb Tense* card, or make an error, play passes to the next student.
10. Play continues until a player has no more cards left.

Variation:
- You can limit the verb tenses used in the game by eliminating one or more of the verb card sheets, based on the level and ability of the students.

Talking Tenses – Cards

sings	laughs	talks	sees
sells	puts	throw	shake
build	eat	meet	sleep

ran

began

felt

cried

met

lost

saw

threw

heard

blew

sent

sat

will do	will fly	will park	will think
will come	will find	will hold	will bring
will keep	will ask	will have	will be

Talking Tenses – Cards

has played	has taken	have seen	have talked
has taught	has been	have bought	have flown
has run	has lost	have drawn	have gone

is coming	is beating	is finding	is getting
are leaving	are shining	are leading	are cutting
am having	am eating	am doing	am going

was taking	was seeing	was sitting	was going
were buying	were driving	were eating	were falling
was putting	was telling	were leaving	were making

Talking Tenses – Cards

Change Verb Tense

Change Verb Tense

Change Verb Tense

Change Verb Tense

Change Verb Tense

Change Verb Tense

Change Verb Tense

Change Verb Tense

Change Verb Tense

Change Verb Tense

Change Verb Tense

Change Verb Tense

Getting across the Board

Learning objective: To practise forming the past tense from present tense verbs.

Game objective: To be the first to get across the board by changing the sentences into the past tense. Players make a trail across the board, either horizontally or vertically. The boxes must be touching, e.g.:

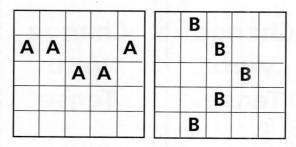

Organization: Played in pairs, or teams of 2–3 players.

Preparation: Copy one board for each pair, or so that two small teams have one board between them.

Description of the game: Hand out one board between two teams. Teams (or pairs) are divided into Team A and Team B. A team wins a cell by calling the block they want (e.g., A2 or C4). One student from the team must then change the sentence into the past tense correctly. If the student is correct, the team may put its letter (A or B) in the block. The other team can challenge if the sentence is correct or not. If one team makes an incorrect sentence, they may not place their letter in the cell. The teacher arbitrates any disputes. Each team tries to get across the board, but also tries to block the other team from connecting their sides. Teams block by winning a cell in the way of the other team's path. In the following example, B wins.

Rules:
1. You may call any cell on the board that does not already have a letter on it.
2. You win a cell by correctly changing the present tense sentence into the past tense.
3. Try to block the other team from reaching the other side of the board.
4. Cells must be touching to form a line across the board.

Variations:
- Divide the class into two teams. Copy the board onto a transparency. Play the game with the teacher acting as monitor.
- Any kind of transformation activity could be written into the blank board.

Getting across the Board

Getting across the Board – Past Tense

	A	B	C	D	E
1	He is young.	Do you know?	I am not going.	They come to the party.	Are you sure?
2	They aren't loud.	I like to play football.	Does she eat chocolate?	Do you drink milk?	He dances really well.
3	Does she play the piano?	Are they busy?	She drives a car.	He studies a lot.	They like music.
4	We watch television.	He is short.	I am tired.	She isn't ugly.	Do you like to play games?
5	I write in English.	I don't drive.	He reads French.	She cooks well.	You don't sing.

Getting across the Board – Template

Getting across the Board

	A	B	C	D	E
1					
2					
3					
4					
5					

Questions, Questions

Learning objective: To recognize verb patterns and practise answering questions in the past, present and present perfect tenses.

Game objective: To match all of the correct answers to the questions.

Organization: Played in pairs, small groups or as a class.

Preparation: Copy a question board and a set of answer cards for each group. This could be pairs, small groups or one board and a set of cards for a class of 28 or less.

Description of the game: Students try to place the answer cards on the question board so the answers match the questions both logically and grammatically. This could be a race to see which team successfully matches all the questions and answers first, but it doesn't need to be a race.

Rules:
1. Place the correct answer cards on top of the questions on the board. Be careful of verb tenses!
2. When you have finished, ask your teacher to check your answers.

Variations:
- Make an overhead transparency of the question board. Work as a class to match all the answers. Cross the questions off the board as the answers are found.
- *Bus Stop*: Give each student an answer card. All students start standing. Read the questions slowly. When a student thinks his/her question has been read, he/she shouts *Stop the bus*. He/She reads his/her answer. If his/her question and answer match, he/she may get off the bus (He/She can sit down).
- Cut the answer cards <u>and</u> the question board so that both sheets are card sets (without a board). Take only enough matching question and answer cards for members of your class. For example, if you have a class of 16, have eight answer cards and eight question cards. These eight questions and answers should match each other. Give the cards out randomly to your class. Students walk around reading their cards until they find their matches. This is a good way to form pairs for another activity.

Questions, Questions

Question Board

1. What did you do last night?	2. Where do you go every week?	3. Where did she go this weekend?	4. Has she been to Europe?
5. Where were you yesterday?	6. What did you do for him?	7. What does she do every night?	8. How many brothers does she have?
9. Where are you now?	10. Where was she yesterday?	11. What time do you eat?	12. How long have you lived there?
13. What has she taken?	14. What do you do every morning?	15. Where have you been all afternoon?	16. What does she do every morning?
17. When did you tell him?	18. What do you do every evening?	19. How long has she lived here?	20. What time does she leave work?
21. Where is she?	22. What did she do for him?	23. Where did you go this weekend?	24. Where does she go every week?
25. Have you visited Europe?	26. What did she do last night?	27. Where has she been today?	28. What classes have you taken?

Questions, Questions

Answer Cards

I called my grandmother yesterday evening.	Every Sunday, I go to my sister's house.	She visited her mother this weekend.	She's gone to France since she was a girl.
I was at the office all day yesterday.	I bought him a cake.	She puts her children to sleep.	She has five!
I'm at home.	Yesterday she was in the beauty salon.	At noon, I eat lunch.	I've lived there for two years.
She's taken the book.	I eat breakfast.	I've been at the doctor's surgery for three hours!	She goes to school every morning.
I told him on Thursday.	I cook dinner for my family.	She's lived here since 2000.	She goes home at 4:00.
She's at the mall.	She made him a birthday cake last year.	This weekend I went to the zoo.	She goes to the gym every Saturday.
I've visited Italy twice.	Last night, she watched television.	She's been at the cinema all day.	I've taken many art classes.

Photocopiable

How Good Have You Been?

Learning objective: To practise answering present perfect questions.

Game objective: To reach the end of the trail by answering questions and following where the answer leads.

Organization: Played in pairs or small groups of 2–4 students.

Preparation:
1. Copy one board for each group.
2. Provide a place marker for each student.

Description of the game: Students begin in the first space: *Have you ever been scared?* If the student says *Yes,* he/she moves his/her marker in the direction of the Y. If the student says *No,* he/she moves his/her marker in the direction of the N.

For lower-level students, simply answering *Yes, I have* or *No, I haven't* is sufficient. For more advanced students, they should discuss each answer, rather than just saying *Yes* or *No.* (Remember that students may begin the answer with *Yes, I have* or *No, I haven't,* but the discussion following the question will often be in the past simple tense.)

Rules:
1. Answer the question in the square. If your answer is *No, I haven't,* follow the arrow with the N to the next question. If your answer is *Yes, I have,* follow the arrow with the Y to the next question.
2. Tell the story of what happened.
3. Be honest. No one is perfect!

Variations:
* After playing the game in class, have students write their own questions on a blank board. Play again with the students' questions.
* Create a class board by asking students what questions they would like to ask their classmates. Brainstorm questions the day before, then provide a game for them the next day by writing their questions on the blank board.

WARNING: This game asks questions that may be taboo in some societies. It is intended to initiate conversation. However, only you as a teacher can determine if the questions are too controversial in your classroom. If this is the case, make your own board, using the blank board provided on page 52.

How Good Have You Been?

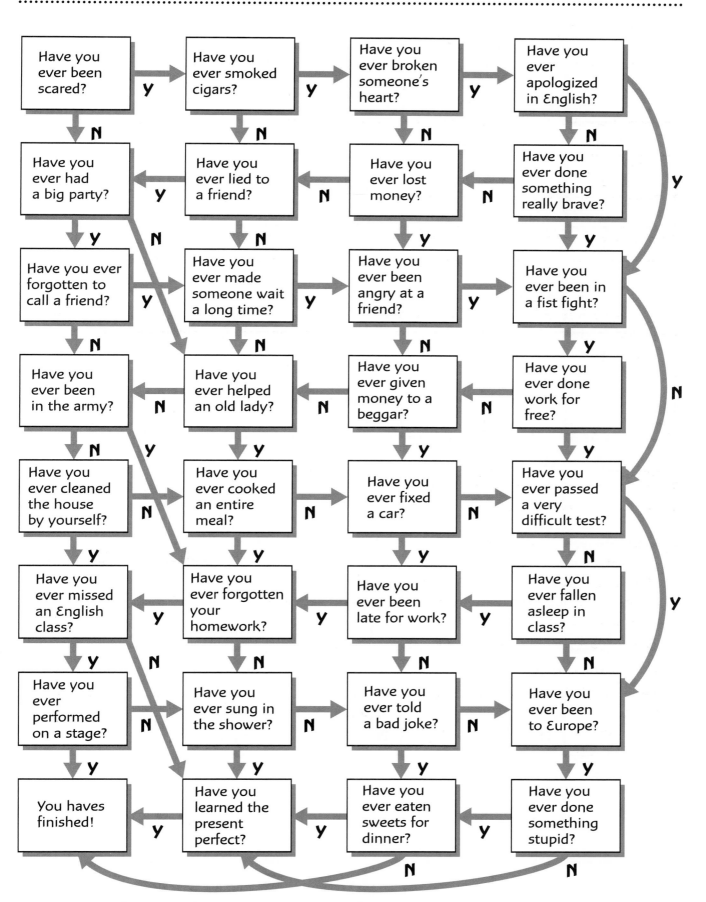

If you don't believe your partner's answer, challenge him or her!

How Good Have You Been? – Template

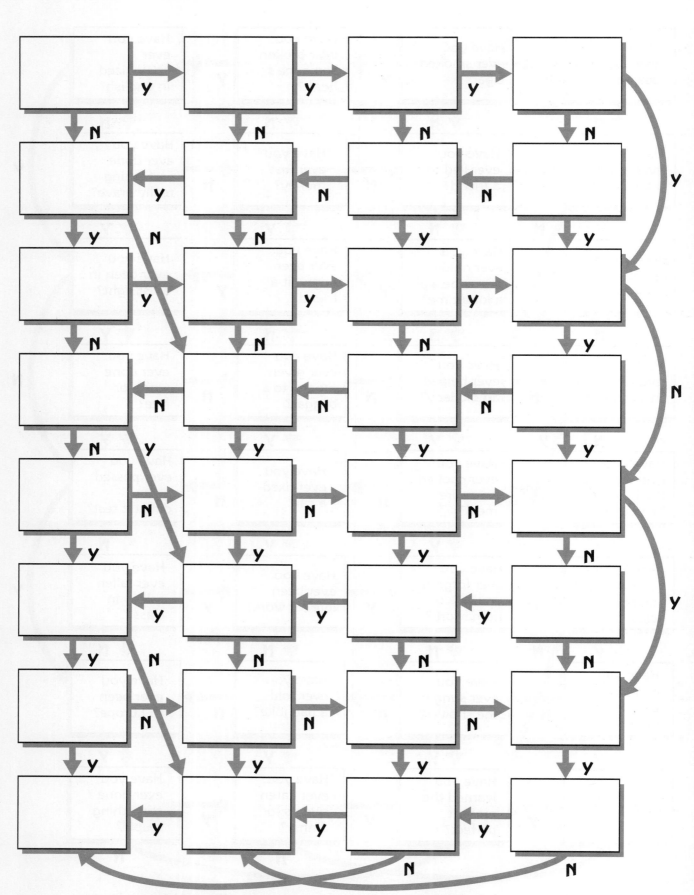

If you don't believe your partner's answer, challenge him or her!

Photocopiable

Spoons

Learning objective: To recognize the correct verb tenses.

Game objective: To collect cards with the correct verb tenses of an irregular verb.

Organization: Played in large groups.

Preparation:
1. Prepare one series of verb cards for each player. (A series of verb cards is the four 3rd-person singular verb tenses for one verb, e.g., *buys, bought, has bought,* and *is buying*.)
2. There are 16 verbs. So if you have 12 players, only prepare 12 series of cards. If you have more than 16 students, duplicate some of the series.

Hint: This game works best with groups of 16 or smaller. For large classes, consider dividing the class into two groups, e.g., for 24 students, divide the class into 12 and 12, and copy two sets of cards with 12 series of verb cards each.

Description of the game: Each large group of students mixes the pack of cards and deals them face down to each student. Each student in the group should have four cards. Students look at the cards they receive and decide which verb they will collect. This may change as the game is played.

At the same time, all students pass one card that they do not want to the left and pick up a new card from the person on their right. All students will have four cards at all times – discarding left and picking up right. **Note:** *It is easier to say Change or Pass at the same time so all students are in sync.*

Students look at their new card and decide if they want to keep it or not. If the student likes it, he/she puts it in his/her hand and chooses another card to pass. If the student doesn't want that card, he/she can keep it and pass another card or pass the same card to the left.

A student tries to get all four correct forms of the verb. When a student has all correct forms of the one series of verb cards, he/she calls out *Verbs* and shows the cards face up for the other students to see. If the student has all four correct forms, he/she wins a point. If the student makes a mistake, he/she loses a point. All other students do not win or lose. The pack is reshuffled and the students play again until one student has five points.

Rules:
1. Do <u>not</u> show anyone your cards. Decide which verb you want to collect. (This may change.) <u>Do not</u> tell anyone.
2. Pass a card you do <u>not</u> want face down to the left.
3. Pick up the new card from the right.
4. If the new card is one you want, place it in your hand and pass another card to the left.
5. If it is a card you do not want, you can keep it or pass it to the left.
6. When you have all four correct forms of the verb, shout out *Verbs*, and place your cards down so everyone can see them.
7. If you have all four correct cards, you win a point.
8. If you have a wrong card, you lose a point.
9. Play again and again until one student has five points.

Variation:

- This game is an educational version of **Spoons**. You can also play it like the game **Spoons**. For each large group, place spoons in the middle of the group. You should have the number of players minus one spoon, i.e. if you have 12 players, you should have 11 spoons. When a student has all the correct cards, instead of shouting *Verbs*, the student takes a spoon. Other students who see this, race to also take a spoon. The student without a spoon loses a point. The person who loses five points is out of the game.

  Note: If a student grabs a spoon first but does not have the correct cards, he/she loses two points.

buys	bought	has bought	is buying
takes	took	has taken	is taking
rings	rang	has rung	is ringing
teaches	taught	has taught	is teaching

sings	sang	has sung	is singing
leaves	left	has left	is leaving
swims	swam	has swum	is swimming
catches	caught	has caught	is catching

says	said	has said	is saying
is	was	has been	is being
breaks	broke	has broken	is breaking
keeps	kept	has kept	is keeping

drinks	drank	has drunk	is drinking
goes	went	has gone	is going
pays	paid	has paid	is paying
sells	sold	has sold	is selling

Gerunds and Infinitives Game

Learning objective: To recognize verbs that require a gerund or an infinitive.

Game objective: To play all of the cards in a student's hand before other students play their cards.

Organization: Played in small groups of 3–5 students.

Preparation:
1. Copy a board and the gerund and infinitive cards for each group.
2. Provide a die for each group and a place marker for each student.

Optional: Copy the rules sheet for each group or put the rules on the board.

Description of the game: Each small group of students mixes the gerund and infinitive cards together and distributes them equally to each student in the group. Extra cards are set aside. Each student places his/her place marker on the Start star space. In turn, each student rolls a single die and moves in any direction, looking for a square he/she can complete using a card in his/her hand. The first parts of the sentences are in the squares on the board. The second parts are on the cards.

The sentence must be correct grammatically, as well as being logical with regard to meaning. For example, if a student lands on *My mother enjoys*, he/she may complete the sentence with *going shopping* or *visiting family*, but none of the infinitive cards are acceptable. Some combinations may be challenged. For example, it is questionable that the student's mother enjoys *cleaning the house*!

If a student lands on a space where he/she is unable to play a card, he/she forfeits his/her turn. The first student to play all of his/her cards wins.

Rules:
1. Start on the star. Roll the die and move in any direction.
2. Complete the sentence by reading aloud the words in the box and choosing one card from your hand. The card must match the box with correct grammar and meaning.
3. If the other students agree that the card matches, place the card in the box marked *Place used cards here.*
4. If you cannot make a sentence with your cards, or your sentence is not correct, you must keep your card and the next student may roll the die.
5. The first student to play all of his/her cards wins.

Variations:

- Add an element of competition. If a student catches another student making a mistake, the student who gave the wrong answer must pick up all the discarded cards.
- There is one board with the answers in the middle of the board and one without.
- You may put your own sentences in the blank board provided in order to practise using gerunds and infinitives that you are studying in your class.

  Note: This may mean you have to change some of the gerund and infinitive cards to ensure the sentences are logical in meaning.

Gerunds and Infinitives Game – Rules

Gerunds and Infinitives Game

This game is for 3–4 people.

1. Mix and give an equal number of cards to each person.

2. Start on the ★. Roll the die and move in any direction.

3. Complete the sentence by reading aloud the words in the box and choosing one card from your hand. The card must match the box with correct grammar and meaning.

4. If the other students agree that the card matches, place the card in the box marked *Place used cards here.*

5. If you cannot make a sentence with your cards, or your sentence is not correct, you must keep your card and the next student may roll the die.

6. The first student to play all of his/her cards wins.

This game is for 3–4 people.

1. Mix and give an equal number of cards to each person.

2. Start on the ★. Roll the die and move in any direction.

3. Complete the sentence by reading aloud the words in the box and choosing one card from your hand. The card must match the box with correct grammar and meaning.

4. If the other students agree that the card matches, place the card in the box marked *Place used cards here.*

5. If you cannot make a sentence with your cards, or your sentence is not correct, you must keep your card and the next student may roll the die.

6. The first student to play all of his/her cards wins.

Photocopiable

Gerunds and Infinitives Game

Gerunds and Infinitives Game

You should consider

The lady prefers

I can't afford

I avoid

Give one card to the person on your left.

The student forgot

My cousin offered

My father learned

I don't mind

My brother hates

My mother enjoys

My best friend promised

My aunt plans

The writer needs

My brothers stopped

My sister wants

Let's start

I suggest ☆

The students decided

The class will continue

My parents recommend

PLACE USED CARDS HERE

The teacher will try

The large group expects

The workers finished

Give one card to the person on your right.

I like

My uncle hopes

Gerunds and Infinitives Game

PLACE USED CARDS HERE	**I suggest** ⭐	**My aunt plans**	**My brother hates**	**My cousin offered**	**You should consider**	
	The students decided				**The lady prefers**	
The teacher will try	**The class will continue**	**The writer needs**	**My mother enjoys**	**My father learned**	**I can't afford**	
	Words that take infinitives: *decide, offer, try, need, learn, afford, plan, hope, expect, promise, forget*				**I avoid**	
	Words that take gerunds: *enjoy, consider, finish, suggest, avoid, recommend, mind*				Give one card to the person on your left.	
The workers finished	Words that take either gerunds or infinitives: *like, hate, start, prefer*					
Give one card to the person on your right.		**Let's start**	**My best friend promised**	**I don't mind**	**The student forgot**	
I like	**My parents recommend**					
My uncle hopes	**The large group expects**					

64

Photocopiable

Gerunds and Infinitives Game – Template

Gerunds and Infinitives Game

PLACE USED CARDS HERE

Photocopiable 65

Gerunds and Infinitives Game

to work.	to drive a car.	to go to the movies.	to go home late.	to visit my family.
to study English.	to clean the house.	to write a paper.	to call a friend.	to read a book.
to swim.	to eat French food.	to have a meeting.	to help my mother.	to have a party.
to go shopping.	to cook dinner.	to buy a new jacket.	to do homework.	to ride a bicycle.

Photocopiable

Gerunds and Infinitives Game – Cards

Gerunds and Infinitives Game

working.

driving a car.

going to the movies.

going home late.

visiting my family.

studying English.

cleaning the house.

writing a paper.

calling a friend.

reading a book.

swimming.

eating French food.

having a meeting.

helping my mother.

having a party.

going shopping.

cooking dinner.

buying a new jacket.

doing homework.

riding a bicycle.

A Ladder Was Taken

Learning objective: To practise forming passive and active voice sentences.

Game objective: To be the first to reach the end of the board (space 40).

Organization: Played in small groups of 3–5 students.

Preparation:
1. Copy one board for each group.
2. Provide a die for each group and a place marker for each student.

Description of the game: Students place their place markers on the Start arrow. In turn, each student rolls the die and moves along the board. If a student lands on a grey square (odd numbers), he/she must make an active voice sentence. If he/she lands on a white square (odd numbers), he/she must make a passive voice sentence. If a student lands on a square with the top of a snake, he/she must follow the snake to the lower square. If a student lands on a square with the bottom of a ladder, he/she may follow the ladder to the higher square <u>if</u> he/she makes a correct active voice sentence. If a student forms an incorrect sentence at any time and the other students "catch" him/her, he/she must start again on the Start arrow. The first student to reach square number 40 and make a correct sentence wins.

Rules:
1. Begin on the Start arrow. Roll the die and move the number on the die.
2. Make a sentence from the words on the board. If you land on a grey square, make an active voice sentence. If you land on a white square, make a passive voice sentence.
3. If you land on a snake, follow the snake down to the lower square.
4. If you land on a ladder, you may follow the ladder up <u>if</u> you make a correct sentence.
5. If you make a wrong sentence, move your place marker back to Start. Check the other students' sentences. If they are wrong, send them back to Start!

Variations:
- Specify a particular tense as well as active and passive voice. For example, only past tense active and passive voice sentences.
- Use the blank board to write your own words. Use the board for other types of sentences.

A Ladder Was Taken

this activity (finish) **40**	You stole thet money! **39**	race (win) quickly **38**	Emma (cook) dinner **37**	both computers (sell) **36**
Lorna (sing) a short song **31**	the puzzle (finish) **32**	Richard (receive) a letter **33**	the play (show) in the city **34**	You lost t the key! **35**
the classroom windows (close) **30**	Sandy (solve) the problem **29**	a prize (earn) **28**	the teacher (teach) the class **27**	a book (write) **26**
you (finish) the puzzle **21**	Barb and Bob (marry) **22**	Sue (take) chocolate **23**	the key (lose) **24**	Paula (drive) the bus **25**
a loud noise (hear) **20**	Dawn (drink) the milk **19**	the washing machine (fix) **18**	Pat (take) photos **17**	the lights (turn on) **16**
Mona (run) a race **11**	the door (open) **12**	Yout broke the glass! **13**	painting (draw) in 1760 **14**	Yout (write) a book **15**
a poem (read) aloud **10**	Jenny (brush) her hair **9**	English (speak) here **8**	Randy (play) music **7**	money (steal) **6**
you (earn) a prize **1**	the last piece of cheese (eat) **2**	Chris (give) a speech **3**	a glass (broke) **4**	Dave (throw) a ball **5**

START →

Photocopiable 69

A Ladder Was Taken – Template

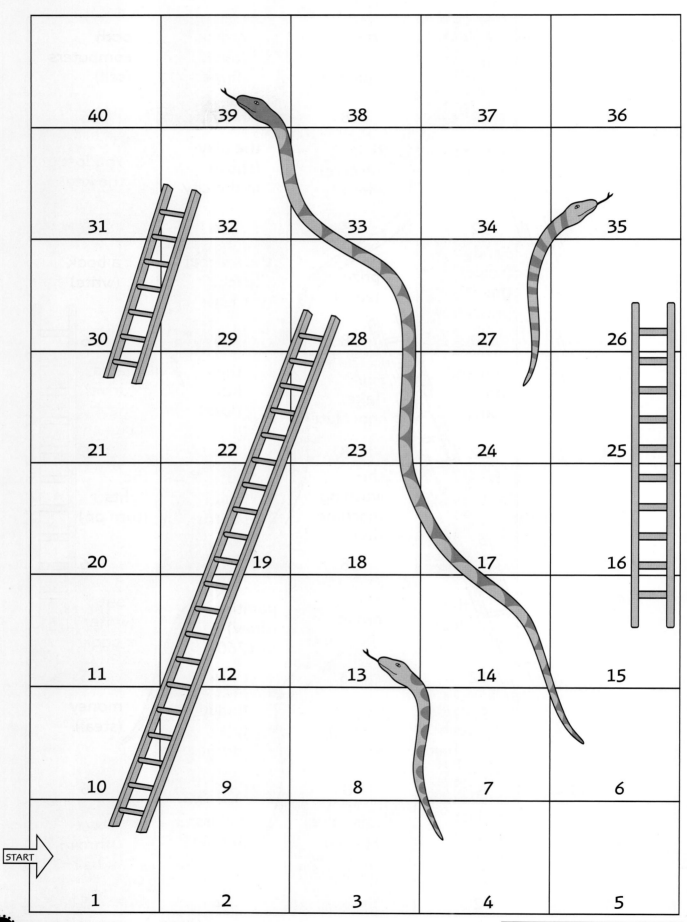

Preposition Pyramid

Learning objective: To practise making sentences using a variety of prepositions correctly.

Game objective: To claim the most prepositions in the pyramid by using each one correctly in a sentence.

Organization: Played in small groups of 3–4 students.

Preparation:
1. Copy one Preposition Pyramid board for each group.
2. Provide three or four different coloured pencils for each group, one for each student.

Description of the game: In turn, each student selects a preposition on the game board and composes a sentence using that preposition. If the sentence is correct, the student claims that triangle, colouring it with his/her colour. Play continues in turn until all the prepositions in the pyramid have been claimed.

Rules:
1. Only one student plays at a time.
2. In turn, select a preposition on the game board and compose a sentence using that preposition.
3. If the sentence is correct, claim that triangle by colouring it in with your coloured pencil. If the sentence is incorrect, you cannot claim the preposition triangle.
4. The other players judge the correctness of the use of the preposition in the sentence. If there are any disputes, the teacher will judge.
5. After each turn, play passes to the next student.
6. The player with the most triangles coloured is the winner.

Variation:
- Make a pyramid with adjective + preposition and verb + preposition combinations (e.g., *full of, afraid of, connect to, apply for*).

Preposition Pyramid

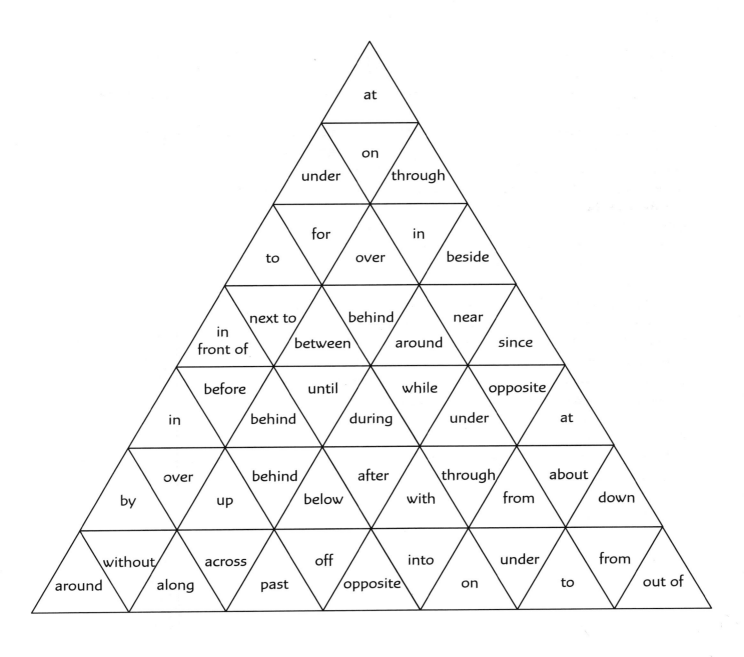

Places, Places!

Learning objective: To display knowledge of prepositions of place by creating a sentence using a noun-preposition combination that fits with a location on the game board.

Game objective: To be the first player to arrive at the Finish square or to use all his/her cards.

Organization: Played in small groups.

Preparation: Provide one deck of cards, a die and a game board for each group and a place marker for each student.

Description of the game: The deck of cards is shuffled and each player receives eight cards (a mix of noun and preposition cards). In turn, the students throw a die and move the corresponding number of spaces. They then try to make a sentence using a noun card and an appropriate preposition card with the location on the board. If the sentence is correct, the student takes two new cards from the deck and play passes to the next student. If the sentence is incorrect, or a logical sentence cannot be made, the student takes two additional cards from the deck as a penalty. Play continues until a player reaches the Finish square, until all the cards have been played, or until no further sentences can be created.

Rules:
1 Sit in a circle with the game board in the middle.
2. Deal eight cards to each player.
3. The first student to play rolls a die and moves the corresponding number of spaces and tries to make a sentence using two of the cards in front of him/her.
4. If you make a correct sentence, take two new cards from the deck. If your sentence is incorrect, take two additional cards as a penalty.
5. Play continues until a player reaches the Finish square, until all the cards have been played, or until no further sentences can be created.

Variation:
• A student can use multiple cards in one sentence to decrease the number of cards in his/her hand.

Places, Places!

15.1

Places, Places!

table · car · train · tent · cinema · bank · room · club

mall · **?** · bench · **?** · **Where?** · **?** · coast

fence · desert · tree

lake · hotel · street · theatre

garden · **?** · desk · **?** · **Where?** · computer lab

library · garden · park · zoo · mountain · valley · swimming pool

path · beach · sea · school · bookshelf

boat · **?** · bridge · car park · **?** · forest

Where? · doctor's surgery/office

pool · **?** · beauty salon · restaurant · aeroplane

police station · **?** · ocean · **?** · ceiling

hospital · **?**

shop · dentist's surgery/clinic · bakery · chair · house · bus · office · Start Finish

Photocopiable

75

Places, Places!

beside	behind	by	at	next to
near	across from	below	on	under
at	next to	in front of	in	over
on	under	above	through	beside
in	over	opposite	with	near

Places, Places!

assignment	watch	class	pencil	coffee
dictionary	clock	family	cafeteria	bookshop
lorry	TV	friend	duck	notebook
bread	knife	bowl	cup	coffee-pot
computer	cow	mouse	monkey	water

Places, Places! – Cards

Places, Places!

sand	camel	baby	car	people
teacher	boat	food	tree	money
girl	boy	light	flower	fish
lion	dog	woman	cat	bird
book	desk	student	man	lemonade

Photocopiable

Places, Places!

Suffix Staircase

Learning objective: To build correct extended words by adding suffix(es) to root words.

Game objective: To be the first player to use all of his/her suffixes correctly.

Organization: Played in groups of 3–4 students.

Preparation:
1. Copy a game board and a sheet of suffixes for each group.
2. Provide a glue stick for each group.
3. The suffix sheets can be cut into strips for each student, if desired, and the students can separate them further during the playing process if you provide them with scissors. (The suffixes can be printed on label paper, if the teacher wishes the students to be able to stick them directly onto the staircase playing board.)

Description of the game: In turn, each student uses a suffix to create a new word on the game board. The suffix must create a recognized word, spelled correctly. Multiple suffixes can be played if they create an appropriate combination. For example, *environ + ment + al + ly* would be acceptable combinations, if the spaces on the game board allow them. Play continues until all the spaces on the board are filled, or until no further suffixes can be played.
Note: Some base words have underlined letters at the end, to indicate that a letter(s) has to be changed or dropped before a suffix is added to make a longer word.

Rules:
1. Only one student plays at a time.
2. You must add a suffix to an existing word to make a correct word.
3. Multiple suffixes can be played on a root word in further turns, if appropriate.
4. The other players judge the correctness of the match on the suffix board. The teacher can judge, if necessary.
5. If a placement is correct, stick the suffix onto the game board.
6. If a placement is incorrect, you must withdraw the played suffix, and play passes to the next student.
7. Play continues until a player uses the last of his/her suffixes.

Suffix Staircase

FINISH

train	play	question	pay	educate	differ

environs, govern, alphabet, assign, situate, log

care, happy

employ, play, refer, process

wonder, beauty

import, usual

art, object

colour, read

discuss

teach

-or	-ence	-al	-ed	-ant	-tion	-less	-able	-ic	-ful
-or	-ence	-al	-ed	-ant	-tion	-less	-able	-ic	-ful
-or	-ence	-al	-ed	-ent	-tion	-less	-able	-ic	-ful
-or	-ence	-al	-ed	-ent	-tion	-less	-able	-ic	-ful
-or	-ence	-al	-ed	-ent	-tion	-less	-able	-ic	-ful
-er	-ment	-ness	-ly	-ent	-ee	-sion	-ily	-ist	-ible
-er	-ment	-ness	-ly	-ance	-ee	-sion	-ily	-ist	-ible
-er	-ment	-ness	-ly	-ance	-ee	-sion	-ily	-ist	-ible
-er	-ment	-ness	-ly	-ance	-ee	-sion	-ily	-ist	-ible
-er	-ment	-ness	-ly	-ance	-ee	-sion	-ily	-ist	-ible

Photocopiable

Suffix Staircase – Template

Suffix Staircase

FINISH

Picking Parts of Speech

Learning objective: To recognize the part of speech of a word based on common suffixes.

Game objective: To claim the most boxes on the board by correctly identifying the part of speech of words.

Organization: Played in pairs or small groups of 2–4 students.

Preparation:
1. Copy a board for each group.
2. Provide a die for each group.

Description of the game: Students take turns rolling a die. If the die shows 1 or 4, the student can claim any unclaimed box with a noun. If the die shows 2 or 5, the student can claim any unclaimed box with an adjective. If the die shows 3 or 6, the student can claim any unclaimed box with an adverb. A student claims a box by correctly identifying a word on the board with the part of speech required and writing his/her name in the space with the correct part of speech. After all the boxes have been claimed, count up the names in the boxes. The person with the most boxes wins.

Rules:
1. If you think another student's choice is incorrect, challenge him/her.
2. If the player is wrong about the part of speech, no student may write his/her name in that box in this turn, and the first student may <u>not</u> choose another box. The turn is finished and the next player rolls.
3. If the student rolling the die cannot find any more boxes with the part of speech needed, the turn is finished and the next student rolls.

Variation:
• A blank board is provided to write words containing the suffixes you have studied in class.

Picking Parts of Speech

1. Take turns rolling a die. If the die shows 1 or 4, you can win any unmarked box with a noun. If the die shows 2 or 5, you can win any unmarked box with an adjective. If the die shows 3 or 6, you can win any unmarked box with an adverb.

   noun

   adjective

   adverb

2. Write your name in every box you win.

3. If you are wrong about the part of speech, you cannot write your name in the box, or any other box. Your turn is finished.

4. The player with the most boxes wins.

quickly	edible	discussion	never	possible	careful
observant	entrance	seasonal	essence	worker	completely
actor	experiment	probably	optimist	reasonable	laziness
painless	always	distant	easily	happily	bravely
usually	capable	operator	reliable	transition	ornament
nation	carefully	efficient	often	sadness	important

Photocopiable

Picking Parts of Speech

1. Take turns rolling a die. If the die shows 1 or 4, you can win any unmarked box with a noun. If the die shows 2 or 5, you can win any unmarked box with an adjective. If the die shows 3 or 6, you can win any unmarked box with an adverb.

noun

adjective

adverb

2. Write your name in every box you win.

3. If you are wrong about the part of speech, you cannot write your name in the box, or any other box. Your turn is finished.

4. The player with the most boxes wins.

Photocopiable

POS-ominoes

Learning objective: To display knowledge of parts of speech by correctly matching like words.

Game objective: To be the first player to lay down all of his/her triangles correctly.

Organization: A group of 4–5 students is best for the game, to maximize the number of turns and allow for adjudication of student answers, but you can work with a smaller or larger group, if desired.

Preparation: You can use the standard triangles provided (which include all the major parts of speech) or have the students create their own, using the triangle template provided.
Note: If the students are creating their own set of playing triangles, this step must be completed first.
Provide each student with six triangles. On each triangle are three different parts of speech, one on each edge, facing out. For example, one triangle might contain a verb, a noun and an adjective; another might have a noun, a preposition and an adverb. The number of parts of speech you choose to include is your choice, based on the level of your students.

Description of the game: The students sit in a circle. Each student has six triangles, with a different part of speech written along each edge. In turn, the students lay down triangles, matching the parts of speech that touch. A noun can be laid next to another noun, a verb to a verb, etc. A triangle can only be inserted into a spot touching two or more sides if the matches are correct on all sides. A match can be challenged by another student; if it is incorrect, the triangle is withdrawn and play passes to the next student. Play continues until all triangles have been played.

Rules:
1. The first student to play lays down any triangle.
2. In turn, each player lays down a triangle against the existing triangles so that the words that touch are the same part of speech.
3. If a triangle touches more than one other triangle, all the touching words must be identical parts of speech.
4. The other players judge the correctness of the match in the triangle placement. (The teacher can judge, if necessary.)
5. If a placement is incorrect, the student withdraws the played triangle, and play passes to the next student.
6. Play continues until the last triangle is played.
7. When all the groups are finished, groups change places and each group reviews the matches made by another group. If they find errors, any triangles following from wrong matches are removed from the game.
8. The group with the fewest removed triangles is the winner.

Variations:

- You can restrict the parts of speech used in the game.
- You can either make triangles with a restricted number of parts of speech or have the students create their own set, based on their level and ability.

POS-ominoes – Triangles

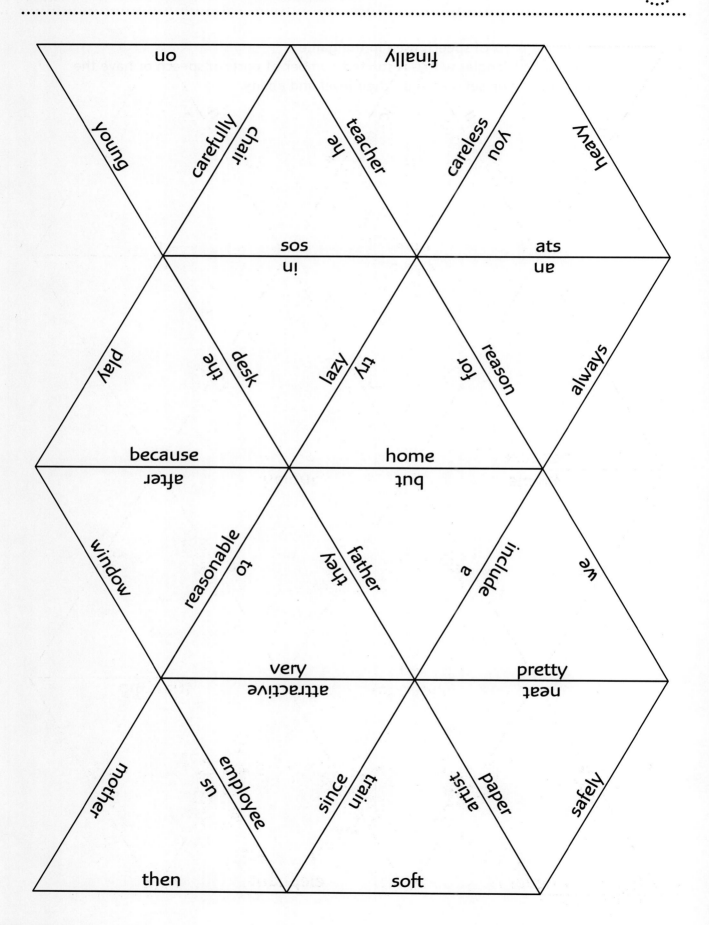

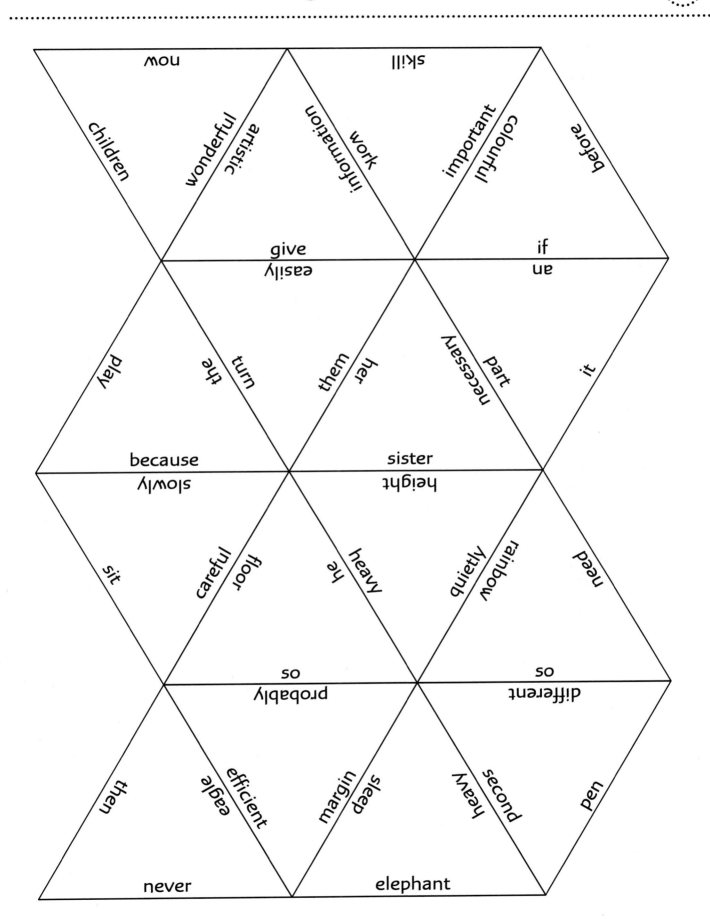

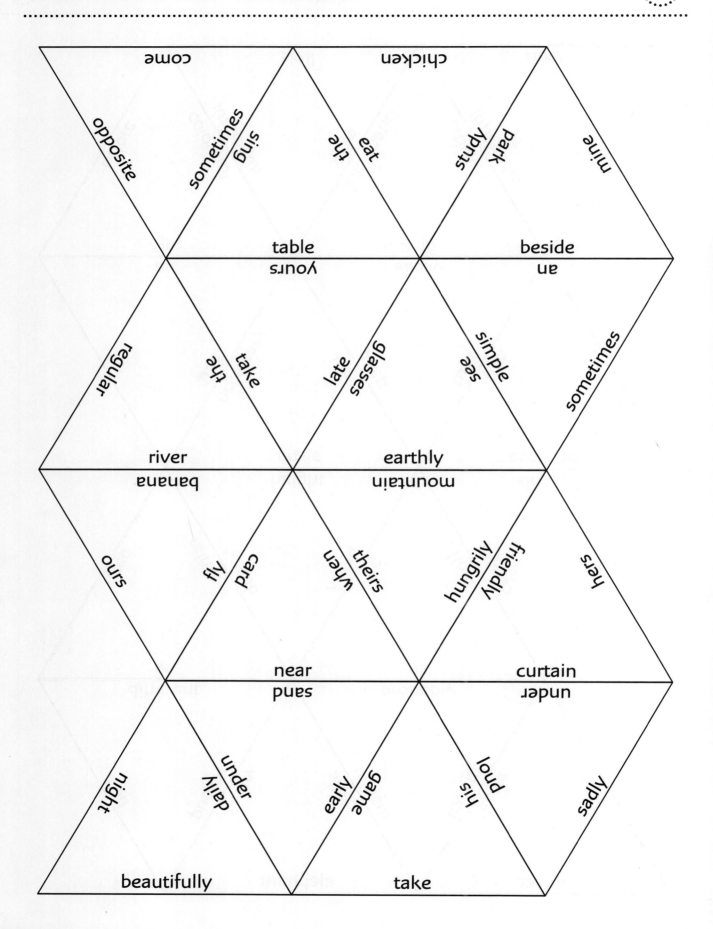

POS-ominoes – Template

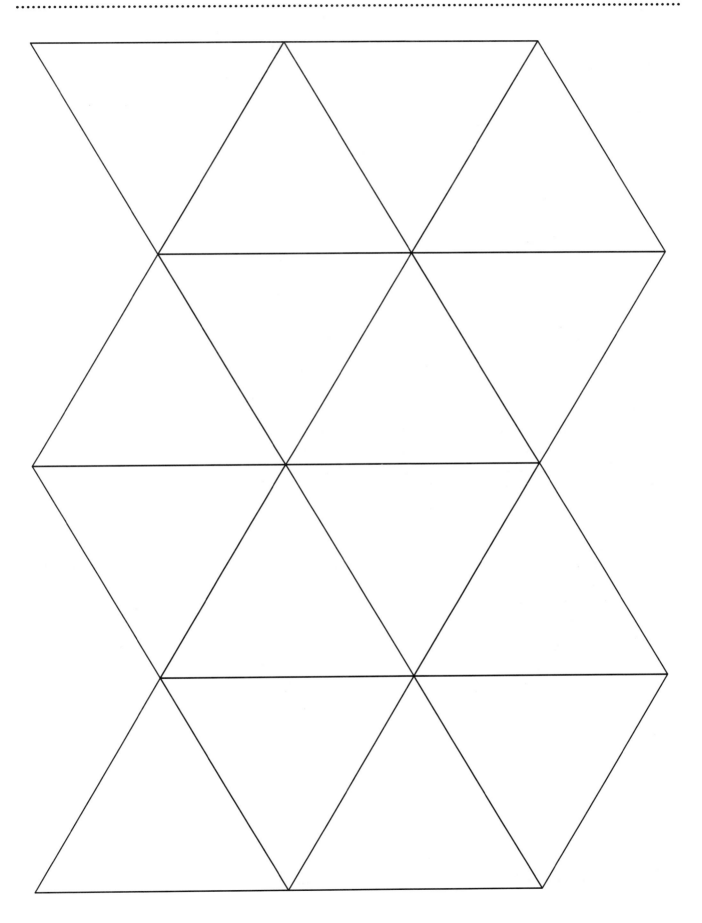

Count and Non-Count Noun Race

Learning objective: To recognize count and non-count nouns.

Game objective: To be the first player to correctly navigate the game board from Start to Finish, identifying count and non-count nouns, as required.
Note: A few of the nouns can be count or non-count, depending on the context. Students should be able to justify their choices.

Organization: Played in small groups.

Preparation:
1. Copy one game board for each group.
2. Provide a coin for each group and a place marker for each student.

Description of the game: In turn, each student flips the coin. If the coin lands on "heads", the student moves his/her place marker to the first count noun from the Start position. If the coin lands on "tails", the student moves his/her place marker to the first non-count noun from the Start position. Subsequent play continues around the game board until the first student reaches the Finish position.

Rules:
1. In turns, flip the coin to see if it lands on "heads" or "tails". Each toss is one turn.
2. If the coin lands on "heads", move your place marker to the <u>first</u> count noun from the Start position. If the coin lands on "tails", move your place marker to the <u>first</u> non-count noun from the Start position. Play passes to the next player.
3. You can challenge any move you feel is incorrect. (For example, someone may have selected the incorrect type of noun, or missed an earlier one of that type on the path.) If the challenge is correct, the player making the error <u>must go back to the Start</u> and the other players continue to play.
4. Play continues around the board. Players can choose the path they wish to take, around the outside of the board or through the middle.
5. The first player to reach the Finish position is the winner.

Variation:
• With more advanced students, each player is required to make a sentence using an appropriate <u>quantifier</u> with the count or non-count noun before claiming the square.

Count and Non-Count Noun Race

butter	tree	banana	grass	carrot	pencil	salt
fish						coffee
cheese		bread	plane	tea		vegetable
yogurt		food		juice	hand	people
bean		pepper				sheep
milk		apple		Non-Count?		sugar
potato		vitamin A	store	friend		beef
time				horse		mother
chair		Count?		bus		truth
book	picture	honey		luck		car
rice		teacher	flower	room		cake
glass						number
START / FINISH	paper	sand	sandwich	office	reason	meal

Go Fish or Chicken?

Learning objective: To ask and answer questions with *some* and *any*.

Game objective: To collect the most pairs of cards.

Organization: Played in small groups of 4–6 students.

Preparation:
1. Copy two sets of cards for each group.
2. Mix the two sets of cards together to create one pack with 40 cards (two of each card).
3. Review the grammar for count and non-count nouns, asking and answering *Have you any ...?* or *Have you a(n) ...?*, *I have some ...* or *I haven't any ...*

Description of the game: Each small group mixes the picture cards together and distributes them equally to each student in the group. Students do not show others their cards. Students look to see if they have any two cards that are the same and place them face up on the table for everyone to see. Two identical cards equal one point. One student begins by asking any student in the group for a card. For example, one student asks the person on his/her right: *Have you any milk?* If the student he/she asked has a milk card, that student must answer *Yes, I have some milk* and give his/her card to the first student. If he/she hasn't a milk card, he/she must reply *No, I haven't any milk*. The play goes to the student on the left of the first student, who asks any student in the group for a card. When students match two identical cards, they place them down in front of them and they earn a point. The student with the most points wins.

Rules:
1. Do not show anyone your cards.
2. Ask any student: *Have you any/a/an ...?* Try to find a card that will match a card in your hand.
3. If someone asks you for a card and you have it, you <u>must</u> give it to him/her.
4. When you get two cards that match, place them face up in front of you.
5. You may only ask one person one question in each turn.
6. The student with the most matched cards wins.

Go Fish or Chicken?

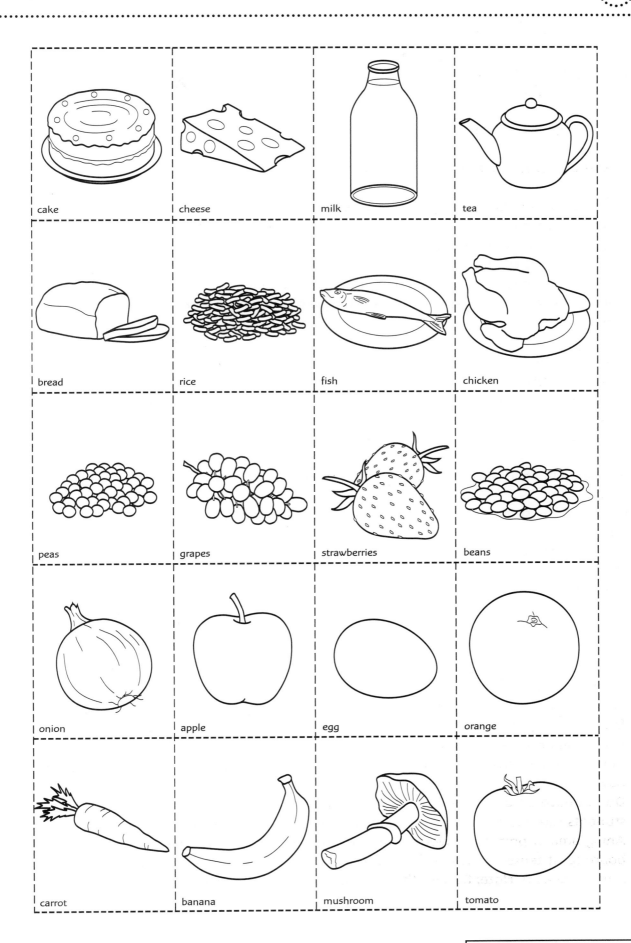

cake	cheese	milk	tea
bread	rice	fish	chicken
peas	grapes	strawberries	beans
onion	apple	egg	orange
carrot	banana	mushroom	tomato

The Tile Game

Learning objective: To distinguish between phrases and clauses.

Game objective: To be the first to reach the end of the trail while asking and answering questions along the way.

Organization: Played in small groups of 3–5 students.

Preparation: Copy one board for each group.

Description of the game: Students write their initials on tiles with clauses on them. All students begin at the bottom of the board (tiles 1–10). Each student chooses one tile which he/she believes has a clause written on it. More than one student can write his/her initials on the same tile. The students climb up the board by choosing another tile <u>next to</u> the tile they wrote their initials on. The tile may be touching diagonally or vertically. Students who make it all the way to the top of the board without ever touching a phrase win. There can be more than one winner.

Rules:
1. Begin by writing your initials on one tile at the bottom of the page (1–10). Choose a tile with a clause on it. More than one student may write his/her initials on the same tile at the same time.
2. Now choose a tile in the next row (11–20) that is <u>next to</u> your tile. You may move diagonally to the left or right, or straight ahead. You <u>must</u> choose a clause.
3. Continue moving upwards, writing your initials on your tiles as you go to the top of the board.
4. When all the students are at the top of the board (61–70), the teacher will tell you which tiles are phrases and which tiles are clauses. If you wrote your initials on any <u>one</u> phrase, you are out. You did not win. Only students who did not write their initials on a phrase tile win!

Variations:
- This game lends itself well to a small class of fewer than 15 students. Photocopy the board onto a poster-sized piece of paper or onto an overhead transparency and play as a class with every student placing a place marker on the tile he/she chooses. Instead of writing initials, students move their place markers up the board. For each row, the teacher tells students who has landed on a phrase and is out of the game. Students who land on a phrase withdraw their place markers and sit aside. They can help other players.
- Divide the class into teams. Play with an overhead transparency and one place marker for each team. Have each team choose a tile in the bottom row (1–10). Play as a team trying to move up the board. At each row, tell students which teams are eliminated because they have chosen a phrase.
- Do not have a trail to the top. Students mark all the clauses on the board. See which students can find all the correct clauses without marking any phrases.
- Any grammar points you would like to distinguish between can be written into the blank board (past tense vs. present tense verbs; grammatically correct sentences vs. incorrect sentences, etc.). **Note:** Be sure there is a possible trail from every "correct" tile!

The Tile Game

The Tile Game

70 looking for a toothbrush	60 the impossibly difficult exam	50 playing this game	40 in front of the large brown house	30 he sat down	20 takes some notes in class	10 she makes desserts
69 the dark and scary night	59 the student studied	49 into the wide open space	39 the bus arrived	29 yellow and white flowers	19 my mother sewed	9 lost his wallet in the street
68 a man swam around the rock	58 an ugly dirty old sock	48 the horse ran away	38 over the weekend	28 I want to go home	18 the thick book with all those	8 the cup leaks
67 a girl is crying	57 with a black magic marker	47 always dancing	37 a phone rang	27 between the blue and white	17 on the first Tuesday of the month	7 she looks in the dictionary
66 the boy in the blue suit	56 the doctor came into the room	46 after a long conversation	36 she came to class late	26 a big piece of blue paper	16 the water froze	6 with an outdated map
65 a colourful kite in the sky	55 in the newly-painted classroom	45 the shoe dropped	35 before the teacher's desk	25 the dog barks at the postman	15 cooks dinner very well	5 this computer works
64 walking in the sunshine	54 talking to a new person	44 the really pretty woman	34 caught in the middle	24 riding the bicycle in the street	14 she played the piano	4 the girl dreams of horses
63 after this class	53 the music is loud	43 Chris laughed	33 on the telephone with his mother	23 among the tall trees	13 a picture of my great aunt's cat	3 next to the busy grocery store
62 the bird flies north	52 waits in a bus station	42 the dessert is sweet	32 doing the homework every day	22 the house is small	12 the door closed	2 by the water fountain
61 a girl with long hair	51 writes a long paragraph	41 reads a new story every day	31 Tom typed the letter	21 Bill with the moustache	11 the young man danced	1 the group travelled to China

The Tile Game

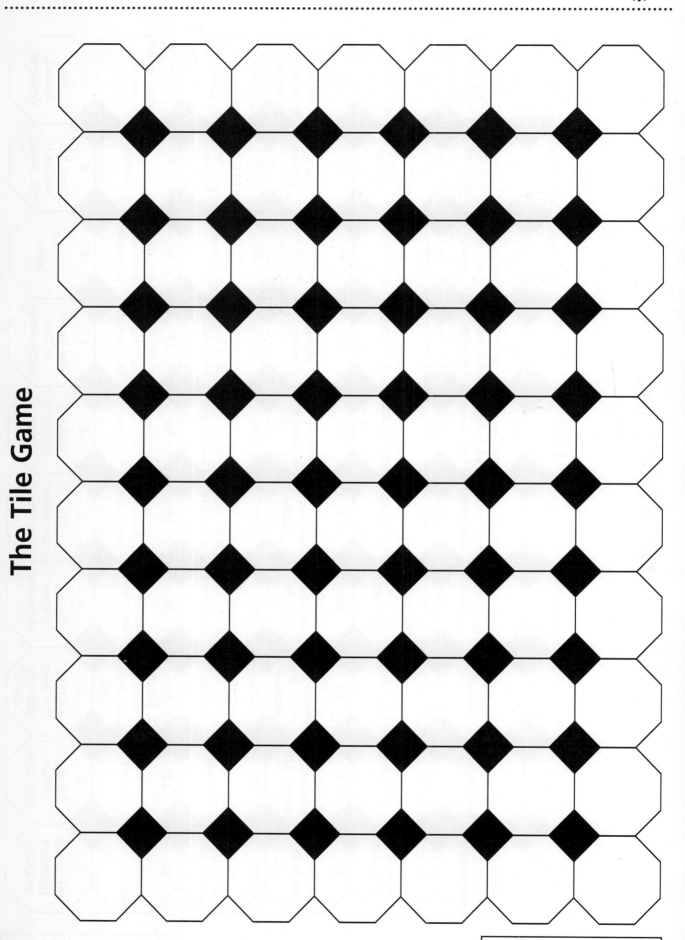

Photocopiable

Pronoun Patterns

Learning objective: To practise placing the correct pronoun in a sentence.

Game objective: To be the first to place all of the dominoes correctly by matching the correct pronoun for the blank in the sentence.

Organization: Played in pairs or groups of three students.

Preparation: Copy and cut up a set of dominoes for each pair or group.

Note: There are different sheets of dominoes depending on which version you are playing.

Description of the game: Students in pairs or groups of three mix the dominoes and deal them out until there are no more dominoes left. The player to the left of the dealer places one domino on the table face up. The player to the right places a domino from his/her hand to match the domino played. This can either be placing a pronoun that will fit in the sentence on the already-played domino, or placing a sentence that will take the pronoun shown on the already-played domino. If the player cannot play a domino next to a played domino, he/she can play the domino vertically.

For example:

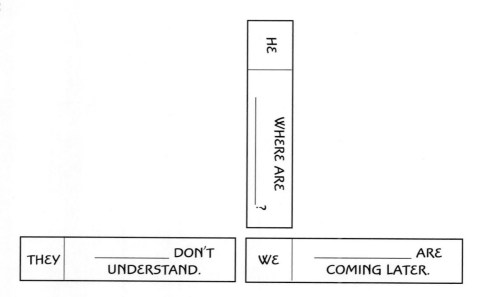

Students play until one student has played all the dominoes in his/her hand. The teacher confirms if all the plays are correct. If there are any mistakes, the group plays again or tries to find and fix the mistake.

Rules:
1. Place a domino from your hand that will match a domino already placed on the table. You can either place a pronoun that will fit in the sentence on the already-played domino, or place a sentence that will take the pronoun shown on the already-played domino.
2. If you cannot place a domino next to a played domino, you can place the domino vertically.

Variations:

- Give each pair or small group only 28 dominoes – only subject + object dominoes (2 sheets), or only possessive pronouns + possessive adjectives (2 sheets) to practise only those distinctions.

- Give each group 42 dominoes – the first sheet of subject + object dominoes, the first sheet of possessive pronouns + possessive adjectives, and the sheet of transition dominoes to practise all of those forms.

- When playing as pairs, give each player different coloured dominoes. (Copy one sheet on pink and the other sheet on green, for example.) Then you can determine which students placed their dominoes correctly.

Pronoun Patterns – Subject + Object Pronouns

HE	_____ ARE COMING LATER.	SHE	ARE YOU TALKING TO _____?
THEY	_____ DON'T UNDERSTAND.	ME	_____ IS MY NEW CAR.
I	PLEASE VISIT _____ NEXT WEEK.	IT	_____ ARE HAPPY TO BE HERE.
US	ARE _____ A DOCTOR?	WE	WHERE ARE _____?
YOU	DO YOU KNOW _____?	YOU	SHE GAVE IT TO _____.
THEM	I WILL GIVE THIS TO _____.	YOU	DID YOU TELL _____?
HIM	_____ IS A GOOD STUDENT.	HER	_____ DRIVES VERY FAST.

IT	_____ TALK LOUD.	ME	DO YOU WANT TO COME WITH _____?
I	I SAW _____ GO TO THE MOVIES.	US	THAT BELONGS TO _____.
THEM	HOW OLD ARE _____?	HER	_____ STUDY FRENCH.
YOU	_____ NEEDS HELP.	THEY	_____ DON'T LIKE PARTIES.
SHE	_____ CAN TELL US.	WE	I SAW _____ YESTERDAY.
YOU	_____ WRITES WELL.	HIM	DO _____ LIKE THIS?
HE	PLEASE GIVE IT TO _____.	YOU	PLEASE PUT _____ OVER THERE.

MY	THIS BOOK IS _____.	HIS	IS THIS _____?
THEIRS	HAS ANYONE SEEN _____?	YOURS	WE DROVE _____ CAR TODAY.
MINE	THOSE ARE _____ KEYS.	OUR	THE PURSE IS _____.
HER	TAKE IT TO _____ CLASSROOM.	HERS	DO YOU HAVE _____?
THEIR	DO YOU HAVE _____ MAP?	OURS	IT IS NOT _____.
YOUR	I HAVE _____ PHONE NUMBER.	HIS	_____ ENGINE IS BROKEN.
HER	DO YOU KNOW _____ NAME?	ITS	I BROUGHT _____ COMPUTER.

Patterns – Possessive Pronouns + Possessive Adjectives 22.4

HIS	THAT BOOK IS _____ .	YOURS	EXCUSE ME, I HEAR _____ PHONE.
HIS	I HAVE _____ NECKLACE.	MY	I'M GOING TO _____ HOUSE TONIGHT.
HER	CAN I BORROW _____ BOOK, PLEASE?	THEIR	THAT ORDER IS _____ .
YOUR	THE CHAIR IS _____ .	THEIRS	WE LOST _____ WAY IN THE CITY.
HERS	THIS IS _____ PRICE.	OUR	THE MUSIC IS _____ .
ITS	THAT WATCH IS _____ .	HIS	I KNOW THOSE TICKETS ARE _____ .
MINE	EXCUSE ME, IS THIS SEAT _____ ?	OURS	IS THAT _____ DRINK?

Pronoun Patterns – Transition Cards

HIS	SHE GAVE THE SCHEDULE TO _____.	THEM	IS THIS PENCIL _____?
HER	I INVITE _____ TO MY HOUSE TONIGHT.	YOU	I WALKED TO _____ CLASSROOM.
MY	_____ HAVE A GARDEN.	WE	THOSE CUPS ARE _____.
OURS	HE WILL GIVE THE BOOK TO _____.	SHE	THOSE JACKETS ARE _____.
HERS	_____ IS A NURSE.	HIM	THE COMPUTER IS _____.
YOUR	PLEASE VISIT _____ FOR DINNER.	I	DON'T FORGET _____ UMBRELLA.
MINE	SHE WANTS TO TALK TO _____.	ME	I SAW _____ PICTURES.

Photocopiable

Plural Picks

Learning objective: To display knowledge of plural formation by correctly matching words with their plural endings.

Game objective: To have the most sets of singular-plural card matches at the end of the game.

Organization: Played in small groups.

Preparation: Use the cards provided (which include examples of all the plural variations) or create your own, using the card template provided. Provide each group of students with one deck of cards.

Description of the game: The students sit in a circle. The cards are spread out before them, face down. In turn, a student turns over any two cards, trying to match the singular form of the noun with the correct plural ending required. (If the plural is irregular, there will be a specific matching card with the full form.) If the match is correct, the student takes the cards and plays again. If the match is incorrect, the cards are placed face down again in the same position, and play passes to the next student. (Students must try to remember where specific cards are located so that they can pick them up, if possible.) A match can be challenged by another student; if it is incorrect, the cards are replaced and play passes to the next student. Also, if a student replaces a correct match, another student should not point out the mistake, but try to claim those correct cards on his/her next turn. Play continues until all the cards have been claimed.

Rules:
1. Sit in a circle with the cards spread out in the middle, face down.
2. The first student to play turns over any two cards.
3. If the cards form a correct singular-plural match (a word with a correct plural ending or the correct irregular noun singular-plural forms), you keep the cards and play again.
4. If the match is incorrect, place the cards face down again in the same location. Play passes to the next student.
5. You can challenge a match made by another student. If it is incorrect, the cards are replaced and play passes to the next student.
6. If a student replaces a correct match, you should not point out the mistake, but try to claim those correct cards on your next turn.
7. You must try to remember where specific cards are located so that you can pick them up during your turn, if possible.
8. Play continues until all the cards have been claimed. The student with the most cards is the winner.

Variations:

- You can restrict the plural forms used in the game to those on which you wish to focus. The blank template will allow you to create additional examples, if desired.
- You can play the game as a matching card game like *Go Fish*, distributing eight cards to each student and then have them ask for a specific match or plural ending.

Plural Picks

Plural Picks

Plural Picks

Plural Picks

Plural Picks

Plural Picks

Plural Picks

Plural Picks

Plural Picks

Plural Picks

Plural Picks

Plural Picks

Plural Picks

Plural Picks

Plural Picks

Plural Picks

Plural Picks – Cards

witch	es	dish	es
box	es	bus	es
potato	es	tomato	es
church	es	place	s

Plural Picks – Cards

sandwich	es	address	es
ranch	es	porch	es
monkey	s	radio	s
key	s	banana	s

Plural Picks – Cards

book	s	toy	s
teacher	s	student	s
park	s	paper	s
test	s	mosque	s

Plural Picks – Cards

fly

(y)ies

baby

(y)ies

party

(y)ies

dictionary

(y)ies

city

(y)ies

family

(y)ies

fairy

(y)ies

story

(y)ies

116

Photocopiable

Plural Picks – Cards

fish	fish	clothes	clothes
glasses	glasses	jeans	jeans
pants	pants	shorts	shorts
scissors	scissors	pyjamas	pyjamas

child	children	person	people
foot	feet	tooth	teeth
man	men	woman	women
goose	geese	mouse	mice

Plural Picks – Cards

photo	s	piano	s
solo	s	avocado	s
belief	s	chef	s
chief	s	roof	s

leaf	(f)ves	knife	(f)ves
calf	(f)ves	wife	(f)ves
life	(f)ves	hoof	(f)ves
shelf	(f)ves	elf	(f)ves

23.10

What If?

Learning objective: To form conditional sentences.

Game objective: To use all the cards in correct sentences.

Organization: Played in small groups of 4–5 students.

Preparation:
1. Copy one set of cards (40 in total) for each group.
2. Make example sentences to show the students the range of sentences possible with the cards.

Description of the game: Each small group of students mixes the picture cards together and distributes them equally to each student in the group. In turn, each student thinks of a first or second conditional sentence related to the picture cards. The cards are intentionally vague to allow for many different combinations of sentences. For example, a student can use the rain cloud card and the beach card to say: *If it rains tomorrow, we won't go to the beach.* Or the student can use the beach card and the card of the man eating fish to say: *If he goes to the sea, he will eat fish tonight.* The student can use the picture of the man eating fish and the card of the person in bed to say: *If the fish isn't fresh, he will get sick.* The bed card can also be used with the card of the house at night to say: *If it is night, I will sleep.*

As students play the cards, they place them face up on the table and these cards are finished. If a student cannot combine two cards, he/she may make a sentence with only one card, but then he/she can only place one card down. When a student uses all of his/her cards, he/she is out of the game.

Rules:
1. Use the cards in your hand to make an "if" sentence. Where possible, use more than one card in a sentence.
2. It is possible to make positive or negative sentences. For example, *we will go to the beach* or *we won't go to the beach.*
3. It is possibe to use a card in either half of the sentence. For example, *If we go to the beach, we will read a book* or *If class is cancelled, we will go to the beach.*

Variations:
- This can be a colloborative game. Have students work together in small teams. Each team tries to write sentences using all the cards. The team with the most correct sentences wins.
- Have students use the cards that have already been placed on the table to create new sentences.

What If?

What If?

Photocopiable

Whose Ending Is It?

Learning objective: To determine when to add 's and when to add ' for possessives.

Game objective: To win the most points by being the first team to choose the correct possessive ending and make a correct sentence.

Organization: Played with two teams.

Preparation: Copy and cut the cards so that each student has one 's card and one ' card.
Hint: You may want to mount on cardboard or laminate at least one 's and one ' card.

Description of the game: Warm up by having all students hold up the correct possessive ending as the teacher calls out nouns. For example, if the teacher calls out *people*, every student should hold up his/her 's card. If the teacher calls out *parents*, every student should hold up his/her ' card. If the teacher calls out *Charles*, the students should hold up both the 's card and the ' card. The teacher checks to see all students are holding up the correct card.

Next, the class is divided into two teams. All the 's and ' cards are collected and put away except one of each card, which is left on a desk at the front of the classroom. One student from each team comes forward. The teacher calls out a noun and the first team member to grab the correct possessive ending card wins a point for his/her team. If that same team member can make a correct sentence using that word, his/her team wins another point. All students come to the front of the class at least once. The team with the most points wins.

List of possible nouns: *teacher, mother, parents, nurses, doctor, brothers, sister, people, engineer, father, uncles, aunt, cousins, children, students, neighbours, man, women, friend,* or any proper name. (Members of the class usually like it when you use their names.)

Rules:
Part One:
1. When the teacher calls out a noun, hold up the correct possessive ending card.
Part Two:
1. Each team sends one member to the front of the class at a time.
2. When the teacher calls out a noun, be the first student to grab the correct possessive ending card. If you are first to grab the correct card, you win a point for your team.
3. Make a sentence using the possessive noun you have just made. If it is correct, you win another point for your team.
4. Play until all students have gone to the front of the classroom.

Variation:
• Have students lose a point if their sentence is wrong.

Whose Ending Is It?

'S	'S	'S
'S	'S	'S
'S	'S	'S
,	,	,
,	,	,
,	,	,